Sparking Student Synapses

9–12

Rich Allen dedicates this book to . . .

*My sister, Karen Walden, for meeting life's challenges
with grace, dignity, and extraordinary courage.*

Larry Walden, for holding her hand every step of the way.

Nigel Scozzi dedicates this book to . . .

My ever-proud parents.

An early mentor, Mr. Bob Grant, for his confidence in me.

*My principal, Dr. Tim Wright, for challenging all of his staff to constantly
question how we teach, and for supporting my professional development
with Eric Jensen and Dr. Rich Allen, whose influence continues to inform
my teaching.*

*The amazing staff at Shore school, for their willingness to experiment.
(Keeping it real—it's a Shore thing!)*

*My Geography staff, for their encouragement—I have a great admiration
for you.*

*My two children, Jye and Priscilla, for being the examples of why I love
teaching and for always asking questions.*

*And, finally, my beautiful wife, Danielle, for your saintly patience and
love.*

Sparking Student Synapses

9–12

Think Critically and Accelerate Learning

Rich Allen

Nigel Scozzi

CORWIN
A SAGE Company

CORWIN
A SAGE Company

FOR INFORMATION:

Corwin
A SAGE Company
2455 Teller Road
Thousand Oaks, California 91320
(800) 233-9936
Fax: (800) 417-2466
www.corwin.com

SAGE Ltd.
1 Oliver's Yard
55 City Road
London EC1Y 1SP
United Kingdom

SAGE India Pvt. Ltd.
B 1/I 1 Mohan Cooperative
Industrial Area
Mathura Road, New Delhi 110 044
India

SAGE Asia-Pacific Pte. Ltd.
33 Pekin Street #02-01
Far East Square
Singapore 048763

Acquisitions Editor: Jessica Allan
Associate Editor: Allison Scott
Editorial Assistant: Lisa Whitney
Project Editor: Veronica Stapleton
Copy Editor: Amy Rosenstein
Typesetter: C&M Digitals (P) Ltd.
Proofreader: Scott Oney
Indexer: Molly Hall
Cover Designer: Rose Storey
Permissions Editor: Karen Ehrmann

Printed in the United States of America.

Library of Congress Cataloging-in-Publication Data

Allen, Richard, 1957 Sept. 28-
Sparking student synapses, grades 9-12 : think critically and accelerate learning / Rich Allen and Nigel Scozzi.

p. cm.
Includes bibliographical references and index.

ISBN 978-1-4129-9114-8 (pbk.)

1. Critical thinking—Study and teaching (Secondary)— United States. I. Scozzi, Nigel. II. Title.

LB1590.3.A53 2012
370.15'2—dc23   2011020716

This book is printed on acid-free paper.

11 12 13 14 15 10 9 8 7 6 5 4 3 2 1

Contents

Foreword

The Story of Nigel

This book is a practical guide to help high school educators adapt to a curriculum with an increasing focus on critical thinking. The following story explains how it came to be written and what it covers.

In many ways, Shore School is a dream teaching assignment. It stands on a hilltop in the heart of Sydney, Australia. Walking around its manicured, century-old grounds, you glimpse magnificent views of Sydney harbor. The boys at this private school wear gray suits and old-fashioned straw boater hats. They stand respectfully when a teacher or visitor enters the room; they call their teachers Sir and Miss.

Yet, despite excellent facilities and well-mannered students, Shore has the same basic educational challenges facing every other high school in the developed world: How do you keep digital natives engaged? How do you keep up with the demands of a new and constantly changing curriculum? How do you balance the need to sustain your scores in state-based testing with your goal of delivering a well-rounded education?

In 2006, the biggest challenge facing Shore's Head of Geography, Nigel Scozzi, was the following: How do you deal with the shift in high school curriculum toward critical thinking? State tests were increasingly asking questions that required more than rote learning—students were required to demonstrate that they could think about and apply the knowledge in different contexts. In Nigel's experience, it was as much as his department could do to get students to simply learn all the content—when would they possibly find time to teach the students to think critically about the new information?

With this question at the back of his mind, Nigel attended a brain-based teaching conference in Australia, where Eric Jensen's keynote on "teaching with the brain in mind" was a revelation. For the first time, Nigel heard about smarter, more purposeful teaching strategies—based on how the brain takes in, processes, and remembers information—that could reach a greater number of students faster! Intrigued, he signed up for a 5-day practical course with Jensen Learning in San Diego, led by Dr. Rich Allen.

After a week of learning how to incorporate movement, music, positive emotions, conversation, and memory strategies into his teaching practice, Nigel returned to Australia and rewrote his department's lessons. Taking a fundamentally new approach, he deliberately used what Rich called Green Light teaching strategies, including engagement and memorization techniques, to quickly create student understanding and recall of the topic's core content. His theory was that if he could accelerate the process of getting students to grasp and remember the core content, it would be much easier to build on this foundational understanding and guide his students to develop and demonstrate the critical thinking required in state-based testing.

This is why, three years ago, Nigel's students found themselves attending a very different type of geography lesson. Rather than sitting quietly, listening to lectures and working from the textbook, students were given challenges that got them up, moving, talking, laughing, and thinking. Every lesson had a sound track. Nigel frequently arrived brandishing props or in storytelling mode. Students competed in games based on TV programs or popular sports. And then, once every student had a firm grasp on the core information, they were challenged to think critically about it—to develop lines of reasoning, to test ideas against their own values, and to understand how content related to the real world.

From the students' perspective, the change was met with wholesale enthusiasm. Student surveys mandated by the school revealed overwhelmingly positive feedback—no one was ever bored in geography! As word spread, geography, previously not one of the most popular elective subjects, was inundated with applications. Today, the Shore Geography Department has the highest retention rate of any school in the state; an astonishing 40% of students choose to continue to study geography as an elective subject through their senior year.

Of course, although student enthusiasm for learning is an important measure of educational success, it is not the one that counts in today's educational systems. However, Nigel's new teaching strategy didn't just win over his students; it also delivered outstanding test results.

In 2009, Shore's geography students achieved an average 86.5 in Australia's High School Certificate examinations—12% above the state average and often substantially above their scores in other school subjects. In 2008 and 2009, three of the state's top 10 geography students came from Shore. Today, geography is one of the school's flagship departments, and Nigel has served as the Shore Mentor of Learning and Teaching.

This book came about as a result of Nigel's experience in the mentor's role. Because, as Nigel started to share his strategies throughout the school, he encountered a stumbling block. Although teachers were delighted with the lessons he created, they often struggled to develop lessons of their *own*. As Nigel says, "These are excellent, dedicated teachers, keen to embrace something new, yet they couldn't easily see how to transform traditional, lecture-based content into engaging lessons that would accelerate learning."

To address this issue, Nigel developed a step-by-step process to turn any secondary content into an engaging and highly memorable lesson as well as techniques and practical tips to encourage students in the art of critical thinking. He also adapted a number of Rich Allen's Green Light strategies for the high school classroom to make each lesson more effective.

This book shares these proven processes and strategies with you. Although it also briefly explains the brain-based theories on which they are based, at its heart, it is a practical guide. This book's purpose is to encourage and support you in developing dynamic Green Light lessons that accelerate learning, empower critical thinking, and improve test results. Rich Allen and Nigel Scozzi hope you will have the courage to try out some of these ideas in your high school classroom.

Acknowledgments

The authors wish to thank the following people for their vital contributions to the development of this manuscript:

- Karen Pryor, editor. Yes, you are an astonishingly talented editor, and yet you gave much, much more to this particular project. Thank you for all of the incredibly valuable things you added to every phrase of the writing process. This book truly stands as a testament to your ability to balance a wide variety of details while firmly holding in place the overarching vision. Again, thank you.
- Wayne Logue, illustrator. Your images have never been more powerful and evocative over the course of our 20-year collaboration than they are here. Thank you for adding that critical extra layer of visual impact, which is so vital to so many of our readers.
- Cheryl Dick, researcher. Your work throughout the growth of this project has been nothing less than inspirational. The credibility of this manuscript is very much a product of the work you did with us. For that, we thank you!

We also thank the creative teachers who generously contributed the original ideas for the additional lessons to this book:

J. P. Friend	Rob Gulson	Joel C. Palmer
Derrice Randall	Natasha Terry-Armstrong	John Tzantzaris

Publisher's Acknowledgments

Corwin gratefully acknowledges the contributions of the following reviewers:

Phil Martin
Teacher
Campbell High School
Litchfield, NH

Amanda McKee
Mathematics Teacher
Johnsonville High School
Johnsonville, SC

Michelle Strom, NBCT
Middle School Language Arts Teacher
Fort Riley Middle School
Fort Riley, KS

About the Authors

**Rich Allen, Ph.D.,** is a highly regarded educator with more than 25 years of experience coaching teachers. Founder and President of Green Light Education, he is the author of numerous popular educational books, including, most recently, *High-Five Teaching K–5: Using Green Light Strategies to Create Dynamic, Student-Focused Classrooms* (2011), *High-Impact Teaching Strategies for the "XYZ" Era of Education* (2010), *Green Light Classrooms: Teaching Techniques That Accelerate Learning* (2008), and *TrainSmart: Effective Trainings Every Time,* 2nd ed. (2008). He has shared his dynamic instructional strategies not only in the United States and Canada, but also in such diverse countries as the United Kingdom, Australia, New Zealand, Hong Kong, Singapore, Thailand, Brunei, Russia, Jordan, and Brazil. Dr. Allen is also a popular keynote speaker at international education conferences and works with schools and school districts to embed effective teaching methods into the mainstream curriculum.

Dr. Allen first took to the stage as an off-Broadway actor, before starting his educational career as a high school math and drama teacher. In 1985 he became a lead facilitator for SuperCamp—an accelerated learning program for teens—and has since worked with more than 25,000 students worldwide. Dr. Allen completed his doctorate in educational psychology at Arizona State University, where he studied how the human brain receives, processes, and recalls information—knowledge that informs all aspects of his teaching strategies. The author divides his time between his home in the U.S. Virgin Islands on the sun-kissed paradise of St. Croix and his fiancée's home in Sydney, Australia, where he is learning to be a stepfather. He can be reached at his e-mail address: rich@drrichallen.com.

 **Nigel Scozzi, PGCE,** is the Department Chairman of Geography and has served as the Mentor of Learning and Teaching at Shore School in Sydney, Australia. In this role he is responsible for guiding more than a hundred teachers in their teaching methodology.

Nigel began his teaching career in Great Britain, where he gained a postgraduate degree in Education from Swansea University. Despite having taught for more than two decades, he continues to be inspired by his students and is forever learning new things himself. He brings to his classroom passion, energy, a huge (if sometimes misguided) sense of humor, and a fierce love for teaching.

Nigel lives with his wife and two children on the Northern Beaches in Sydney, where he indulges in his passion for surfing.

1

The Rise of Critical Thinking

Adapting to the New Goals of Our Education System

"Learning without thinking is labor lost; thinking without learning is dangerous."

—Confucius

Around the developed world, high school educators are facing perhaps the biggest curriculum change we have ever witnessed. In the United States, the United Kingdom, Hong Kong, New Zealand, and Australia, the rise of critical thinking as a determinant of success in state and national testing is introducing a new level of challenge in almost every subject. Suddenly, teachers, who are already struggling to get through their content, are finding it is not enough to teach the facts. Students must also be able to use those facts to solve problems, draw conclusions, and form new arguments.

Clearly, curriculum change is not new. For as long as we have had high schools, teachers at this level have had to adapt to an education system that routinely moves the goal posts. Curriculum changes are sparked by any number of factors: new industries requiring new skills, new technologies, and new government advisers. Some are local, and some are global. Some are short-lived, and some are foundational.

The rise of critical thinking is likely to be pervasive and profound because it is being driven by societal and economic change. In the 21st century, we are experiencing exponentially rapid change created by the information age. In a world where students and workers can retrieve any amount of factual information at the click of a mouse, a large proportion of education's traditional rote learning is fast becoming superfluous (Wiggins & McTighe, 2008).

Increasingly, the world's governments are recognizing that the skills required to support productivity in the digital economy are very different from those required in the industrial era. Our 20th-century education systems were essentially designed to turn out factory fodder: workers who showed up on time, had specific skills, and reliably performed rote tasks. Now that Western economies have shifted from manufacturing to services, the skills prized by today's employers are profoundly different. They are innovation, creativity, and critical thinking.

This has created a profound change in the overarching goals of the world's education systems. The Obama administration's Strategy for American Innovation is committed to the following: "Educate the next generation with 21st century knowledge and skills while creating a world-class workforce" (www.whitehouse.gov/administration/eop/nec/StrategyforAmericanInnovation). At the Association of American Colleges and Universities Annual Meeting in January 2010, U.S. Department of Education undersecretary Martha Kanter said: "In today's world, we know that our students will have many jobs and will likely change career paths a number of times, so they have to be equipped for lifelong learning and continuous improvement. We talk about preparing students for STEM [Science, Technology, Engineering, and Mathematics], but they're not going to pass Statistics or Calculus or Freshman Composition, which are gateway courses into STEM fields, without a general education foundation that gives them the critical thinking and analytical reasoning skills to use in whatever field or fields they choose" (U.S. Department of Education, 2010).

This trend is being mirrored throughout the world. In 2010, for the first time, high schools in the United Kingdom began offering critical thinking as a dedicated subject. In Hong Kong, according to the *Basic Education Curriculum Guide* (Education Bureau, 2002), educational priorities for 2001–2006 were "communication, critical thinking and creativity." Since 2008, Australia has been developing a new national curriculum in which the ability to think critically receives special mention in each subject area; see the examples in Table 1.1.

Clearly, critical thinking will be an increasingly important and relevant topic in the world's high schools for years to come. The question for high school teachers is *how* to teach this dramatically new skill to complement their normal subject matter—and how to find the time to do so.

In previous curriculum changes, educators had to include new information, but their teaching strategies could remain unaltered. By contrast, this curriculum change is not in the content—it is in the way students think about the content. In the high schools of the future, learning the core content will merely be the starting point of the teaching process, or Phase One. In Phase One, students will learn, understand, and remember the core content and vocabulary. In Phase Two, they will critically assess, evaluate, and reflect on this content (Swartz, 2008, p. 27).

Although this is already happening in some high school classrooms, many teachers are finding the process extremely challenging. Either they struggle to get through Phase One, leaving no time for Phase Two, or they have no formal training in teaching

Table 1.1

Subject	Australian National Curriculum Syllabus Comments
Math	In a democratic society, there are many substantial social and scientific issues raised or influenced by public opinion, so it is important that citizens can *critically examine* those issues by using and interpreting mathematical perspectives.
English	Students are creative and resourceful and are able to think critically, analyze information and solve problems with the "general capabilities that underpin flexible and *critical thinking*."
History	There is a greater emphasis on skills associated with *critical thinking* and analysis of sources, and the contestability of historical interpretation.
Geography	By using current events to explore geographical questions, students of geography are given practice in *critically thinking* about contemporary issues.

Source: Copyright © Australian Curriculum, Assessment and Reporting Authority. For more information please visit http://www.acara.edu.au/default.asp

critical thinking, or both. This book offers practical strategies that address both areas. It shows educators how to do the following:

1. Teach the material in a *rapidly memorable* way so that you can . . .

2. Devote significant class time to *critically analyzing* this information

You may be wondering about the book's focus on *rapidly memorizing information*. Some might argue that this is simply rote learning, and, in fact, at this level that would be correct. However, facts are the beginning point—without them, there can be no in-depth processing or discussion. When students have no easy way to recall essential information, they spend 100% of their class time on simply remembering, with no time for critical thinking. Instead, if they can quickly recall key information, class time can be devoted to critical thinking opportunities. Simply put: You can't have an informed discussion unless all parties have a basic understanding of the core facts.

Accelerating Core Content Learning

It's time for education systems to accept that, if they require students to become critical thinkers, they must equip teachers with accelerated learning strategies that allow every student to quickly understand and remember core content. This means letting go of the traditional *chalk and talk* approach to education, which is increasingly inefficient and ineffective.

To clarify, chalk and talk is where a teacher's primary mode of information delivery is to stand at the chalkboard—or PowerPoint screen or smart board—write or show information, and then talk about it while students listen, copy the information, and then do a worksheet.

This lecture-saturated educational approach is what we call *Red Light* as opposed to *Green Light* teaching. These terms come from the book *Green Light Classrooms: Teaching Techniques That Accelerate Learning* (Allen, 2008). The central tenet of the book is that lecture-based teaching has never worked well for every student, and certainly doesn't work for the vast majority of the digital natives inhabiting today's classrooms. The book draws its theories from brain-based research that reveals many traditional teaching assumptions—expecting students to usefully pay attention for longer than 10 minutes; expecting teachers to talk more than students; and expecting students to learn when they are feeling stressed—actually *stop* students from learning (hence Red Light) and waste huge amounts of teaching time on fruitless endeavors.

Red Light teaching is the illusion that, if you can get your students to sit quietly while you talk, you are succeeding as an educator. Green Light teaching offers an opposite view. Its premise is as follows: You may have *said* it—and your students may have done a credible job of pretending to pay attention—but if they didn't hear, understand, and remember it, then you didn't *teach* it.

Green Light strategies focus on what works, based on the latest research on how the human brain learns and remembers new information and on the psychology of today's kids. The result is a host of new and creative ways to teach that will restart the learning process, boiled down into nine key strategies:

1. **Memory**   Pegs, association, body location, acrostics, and rhyming

2. **Connections**   Creating meaning; allowing students to own the material

3. **Movement**   Physically engaging students in the learning process

4. **Novelty**   Harnessing something *different* to capture students' attention

5. Tone	Music, chants, teacher's tonal changes, and pauses
6. Emotion	Using laughter and surprise to fire curiosity and excitement
7. Socialization	Student-to-student discussions, processing, and debriefs
8. Drama	Theatrics, story-telling, and students acting out the learning
9. Visuals	Posters, mind maps, doodles, and drawing

Around the world, these strategies have been proven to accelerate learning, reducing the amount of time it takes students to learn the content and increasing the number of students who truly understand it. They are the keys to zipping through Phase One so that you have time for critical thinking.

Defining Critical Thinking

Before we dive into how to teach critical thinking, we must begin by agreeing on a working definition of what that actually means.

As you might expect, education already has a wide variety of definitions of the expression *critical thinking*. Some are simple and use language common to many people. Others are complex and include lots of higher education jargon. Fortunately, many of the definitions share some common themes. For the purposes of this book, we have adopted a working definition that is simple to state and yet underpinned by teachable, learnable, and observable behaviors.

You may feel there is much more to the idea of critical thinking. In fact, we agree. For example, one aspect of critical thinking not stated

Definition

"Critical thinking involves the ability to make appropriate judgments, based on the evidence available."

Teachable and Observable Behaviors

Critical thinkers seek to

Understand the logical relationship between ideas

Assess, appraise, and evaluate various lines of reasoning

Detect inconsistencies, mistakes, and errors in arguments

Identify the relevance and importance of ideas

Reflect on their own beliefs, principals, standards, and values above, yet surely important, is developing one's intellectual humility and intellectual empathy, where one becomes less biased and more open to new perspectives. Or another component might be the need to understand the essential difference between perception and judgment. Although we agree with both of these ideas, the nature of this book requires a steady focus on tangible, and ultimately learnable, concepts and constructs. We believe the five qualities shown in the box on page 6 best meet these criteria.

The Overtesting Plague

As this book addresses curriculum change, we would be remiss if we did not put this change in the context of the blight that is affecting most of the world's education systems: Overtesting has become a plague of epidemic proportions. Although government officials, high-level administrators, and others well-distanced from the everyday classroom applaud the data-driven test frenzy, overtesting has brought forth a landslide of negative reactions from teachers and students alike. Students resist the constant assessment of their skills, failing to see any relevance in the persistent need to test, test, test (Nichols & Berliner, 2008). And teachers decry the need to *teach to the test*.

Overtesting teaches students the *sealed box* theory of education—sealed boxes representing the facts students must learn. The sealed box theory is simple: Teachers show students many sealed boxes. The teacher states that the sealed boxes are very, very important. Teachers show students how to pick up and move the sealed boxes from point A (the textbook/board) to point B (the test paper). Students are primarily tested, and judged, on their ability to move the sealed boxes from point A to point B. Success equals moving those boxes! Move more and succeed better! Become the best sealed box mover in your class, in the school, in the country. Move them—harder, faster! Move more, more! Succeed! Succeed!

This approach to education creates an enormous number of problems, but let us deal with three of the most important.

First, students never learn *why* what's inside the box is important, in any meaningful way; nor do they learn *how* the contents of one box might relate to the contents of another. In this approach to education, although some students become incredibly skilled at moving sealed boxes from point A to point B, this is not a talent of any real use in today's world.

Second, students are sold the erroneous idea that doing well on the test will make them good, successful, and generally worthwhile people. Clearly, this is an unhelpful and demoralizing message for those who don't do well in a Red Light classroom and under test conditions. Nothing stifles lifelong learning like teaching a child he or she's a failure.

But it's also bad for those who do succeed. Overtesting leads straight-A students to believe they've done all that's required to be good citizens and do well in their choice of career. Yet, as any academic graduate in the first few months of a corporate job will tell you, most are woefully unprepared. Organizations don't want young people who know the answers on the test; they want self-starting innovators who are good at working in teams, have strong communication skills, and are adept at solving problems. In this environment, most graduates take a good three months of frantic learning and adjustment before they are able to contribute anything of actual value to a company. For those who believed the education system's claim that the only thing they need to do is pass the test, the experience is extremely sobering.

Third, and perhaps most important, overtesting further undermines the position of teachers in our communities. For many years, teachers were revered by society. We, as communities, handed them our children with one powerful mandate—to help them learn, grow, and mature into responsible members of society. As we are all too aware, this respect for teachers has faded in recent years, and overtesting is partly to blame because it has stripped two crucial responsibilities from the teaching profession.

We used to trust teachers, first, to understand what our kids needed to learn; and second, to decide how best to teach them. But now, since it's *all about the test,* teachers no longer have the freedom to adapt to the needs of their students. Instead, we merely ask educators to teach students *these* facts in *this* way. In some states, teachers are actually given teaching scripts to control the education process down to the spoken word level!

But this approach assumes that all students learn at the same speed and in the same way. In a test-driven environment, teachers are no longer able to make appropriate choices for the students sitting in front of them. They can no longer adjust the ebb and flow of the learning process to maximize the effectiveness of each lesson and unit. And, ultimately, they are no longer able to see students as individuals with unique needs—they must teach to the standard. Power has been wrested from their control for the "greater good" of making all students learn the same thing, at the same time.

In the end, what does this untrusting environment create? It builds a climate of reluctance and suppression, of failure and negative competition, of anger and resentment, on the part of both the teacher and the student.

Perhaps the entire issue of overtesting can be summed up with the following phrase:

> *"A cow doesn't get heavier if we weigh it more often."*

Similarly,

> *"Students don't get smarter if we test them more often."*

That said, let us be clear that *testing itself is not a bad thing*. Used properly, it can accurately assess student knowledge, and subsequently act as a guide for teachers in knowing where to direct future lessons. The current widespread dissatisfaction is the result of testing being done too frequently, and with unrealistic emphasis and importance placed on the results.

Proper testing procedures will always be a part of the educational process, at some level. But we should *not* test students every year, several times, simply to see them perform. And most important, we should *not* let them ever believe that the results of those tests in any way indicate their worth as people. Instead, we should seek to comprehensively revise our fundamental approach to teaching and learning at the secondary level and actively seek to develop those skills in students—teaming, communication, problem-solving, respect for diversity—that they will truly need to succeed in life.

A Starting Point

The approach outlined in this book gives high school teachers a process for designing lessons that both teach facts quickly and help to develop critical thinking. We understand that students will be tested, and the test results will be important. We also understand that people need more than mere facts to succeed in life; they need the understanding and ability to carefully analyze the available information to make the best possible decisions. Although facts are always readily available to students in this current generation, their ability to analyze the data beyond mere memorization will be a significant part of their success.

How to Use This Book

This book is a guide to help secondary teachers develop Green Light lessons that include elements of critical thinking. It's been designed around the idea that many teachers lack the time necessary to read an entire book.

To get the most value out of it, here is a suggestion. Please carefully review the next section, which introduces the five steps to consider when developing your own lessons. Then, just *scan* the section on the suggested translation techniques. Once you have a basic understanding of these techniques, begin to browse through the lessons to see how they are constructed. The subject areas vary greatly, and it may be most useful to begin scanning lessons designed around content with which you are familiar. Familiarity with the content will help free your mind to study *how* the lesson is organized. From there, branch out and peek at other lessons. Soon enough you'll begin to see the consistent, underlying structure to each of the lessons, *regardless* of the content!

Finally, dip into the last section of the book, which tackles four fundamental keys to making engaging lessons more effective:

Recall	Teaching your students memory pegs
Rock	Using music to support activities and learning
Reorganize	Matching your classroom setup to your lesson
Reflect	Setting up productive student conversations

As you implement your new lessons, this might be a section you revisit to find additional tactics to manage what will almost certainly be a more dynamic teaching process.

Why Bother?

Changing the way you teach can be challenging, time-consuming, and downright scary. But, as the thousands of Green Light teachers around the world will tell you, it's worth it. Not only will your students achieve more than they or you could ever have imagined, but you will start to have fun again. If you can reengage your students in the learning process, their behavior will improve, their results will soar, and you will remember why you got into teaching in the first place. Green Light education strategies will allow you to teach beyond the test, giving you the time and influence to teach your students the life lessons they really need to be effective, responsible citizens.

2

The Process

Transforming Core Content
Into Dynamic Lessons

A Little Perspective

Before we start, let's be clear. You don't have to be creative, artistic, or imaginative to design your own dynamic lessons. Nor do you need a flamboyant personality or a dramatic talent to present them. As long as you understand your content and are willing to try something a little different, you can design and present engaging lessons that promote critical thinking in high school students.

If you feel slightly daunted at the prospect of designing a dynamic lesson, that's a very healthy reaction. It's the same reaction we have when it comes to doing anything unfamiliar for the first time, whether it's scuba diving, making a soufflé, or driving a truck. They're all pretty daunting until someone shows you *how*.

Five Steps to Designing a Dynamic Lesson

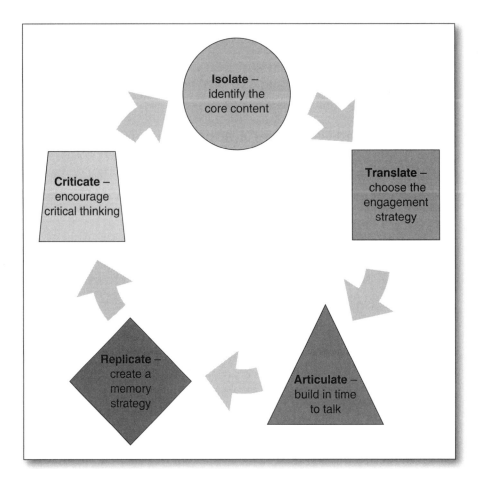

Separate the wood from the trees

STEP 1   Isolate—Identify the core content students need to remember as the foundation information to support critical thinking about this topic.

The first step is to identify the core information you want your students to take away from this lesson. This is likely to include

- **A key concept**: The single most important idea they must understand; may include a procedure, diagram, or process they have to be able to remember

- **New vocabulary**: Any unfamiliar terms they need to be able to use correctly

For example:

Lesson	Key Concept	New Vocabulary
Comparative study of texts in a pair of texts: Sonnets of Barret Browning F. Scott Fitzgerald's *The Great Gatsby* *English*	Understand context of Barrett Browning's *Victorian Age* & Fitzgerald's "Roaring 20s" plus inherent values; ability to demonstrate how shift in context leads to change in values	Binding notions, love, feminism, social mobility, optimism, religion, mutability, values
Different types of angles *Math*	Ability to identify the different types of angles	Right angle, acute angle, obtuse angle, straight angle, reflex angle, angle of revolution, corresponding, co-interior, and alternate angles
Offset surveys (field diagrams) *Math*	Transferring an actual block of land to a field diagram	Field diagram, offsets
Cell—surface area to volume ratio and rate of movement of materials in & out of cells *Science*	Efficiency of smaller cells in exchange of materials Surface area to volume ratio	Surface area to volume ratio, diffusion

(Continued)

(Continued)

Lesson	Key Concept	New Vocabulary
First-, second-, and third-order levels *Science*	Ability to observe a lever & identify as first, second, or third order Position of load, fulcrum, effort in different levels FLE-123	Fulcrum, load, effort
Height on maps *Geography*	Ability to view landscapes in three dimensions	Contour lines, contour interval, aspect
Resilience of ecosystems *Ecology/Geography*	Ecosystems *bounce back* from stresses Dynamic equilibrium curve	Amplitude, malleability, elasticity, threshold, human modification
Business life cycle *Business Studies*	Each business goes through the stages of the business life cycle with identifiable characteristics Business life cycle diagram	Establishment, growth, maturity, postmaturity (decline, renewal, steady state), market share
Marketing—product positioning *Business Studies*	Positioning refers to the perception of the product/brand compared with competitors' products/brands in the mind of the consumer Product positioning matrix	Positioning, competitive advantage, perception
Circular flow of income *Business Studies*	The flow of income in the economy varies according to level of leakages/injections Circular flow of income diagram	Injections, leakages, recession, imports/exports, taxation, government spending, saving, investment, factors of production

Important: This information is the foundation on which everything else depends. This is what you teach in the first part of your lesson—or in the first lesson, if this is a multisession topic. Only this, and nothing else!

Why?

Imagine a friend offers to take you hiking on the weekend. She picks you up and drives to a remote spot you've never been to before. As soon as you arrive, she leaps out of the car and hurries off down a twisty path. You call out to her, but she ignores you. Frightened of getting lost, for the next hour, you scramble over increasingly difficult terrain, with your (soon to be ex-) friend always just slightly too far ahead for you to catch up. Along the way, you pass breathtaking views, but you're too stressed to really appreciate them. Suddenly, just when you think you really can't go on any longer, you round a corner and discover you're back at the car where your friend is unpacking a picnic lunch.

What should have been an enjoyable experience—an hour's circular walk with stunning views before a picnic—turned into a nightmare because your friend didn't tell you where you were going or what to expect. This is exactly what happens to our students when we include too much detail at the beginning of a lesson, as demonstrated in the following case study.

CASE STUDY

The purpose of a math lesson was to teach students to calculate the remaining area when a circle was cut out of a square. The teacher started well. "First we calculate the area of the square," but then started diving into detail: "So, how do we do that? Well, let's look at an example. Suppose . . ." The class was lost within seconds. When asked afterward, half the students said the topic was very tricky.

Next time, the teacher took a different approach. "There are three simple steps to calculating the remaining area: first, calculate the area of the square (A); second, calculate the area of the circle (B); third, subtract B from A." The class relaxed, immediately grasping the simplicity of the idea, and paid attention while the teacher expanded on each part of the process because they knew where this was going. Afterward, every student could recall the concept and thought it was pretty simple.

We need to start teaching every new topic from the perspective that our students can't process or remember details until they grasp the core information. Once they have this in their heads, they can connect new information to it and see those connections.

This is basic schema theory. For decades, cognitive scientists and psychologists have discussed the schema theory of human memory (Ausubel, 1967; Bartlett, 1932; Head, 1920; Piaget, 1926). The core idea is that humans organize new information around their previously developed schemata, or "networks of connected ideas" (Slavin, 1988). In other words, you need to create some mental hooks for your students so that they can hang the detail on them. If you don't create the hooks first, the detail will "fall on the floor" and get lost in the morass of other information your students have never connected with.

Just like items discarded on their bedroom floors, your students will never be able to find this detail again! We need to make sure they have somewhere safe to store it so that they can put their hands on it in seconds.

Nigel's Notes

In my first few years of teaching, I used to spend endless hours preparing my lessons by making copious notes about the topic/chapter to be taught. I rarely gave much thought to the actual core concept I wanted to get over to my students. I was driven by "being ahead" of the students—my notes were a security blanket so that I would not get "caught out." As a result, when I was in the classroom, I frequently got caught up in the detail and would lose track of what it was I was trying to teach. I call this the can't see the wood for the trees *syndrome.*

How?

If you've been teaching your content for a long time, you can probably recite the core information for most topics off the top of your head. If you're teaching something new, or find yourself struggling to let go of the details (left brainers, that might be you!), here are some strategies for isolating your core content. Read the chapter quickly if you need to, and then think about one of the following approaches:

- **Synopsis**—If you could only give your students a 50-word written summary, what would it say? Would you need to explain any of the vocabulary?

- **Discussion**—What information would your students need before they could ask meaningful questions about this topic? What new vocabulary might they need to use?

- **Mind map**—What would a mind map of the topic look like? (You may need to draw one.) The information in the first tier of lines is your core content. For example, the map below shows the first levels of a map describing the ecological study of ecosystems at risk of natural and/or human stresses.

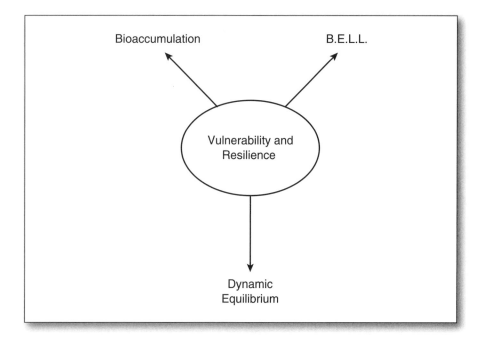

Engage their attention . . .

STEP 2   **Translate**—Choose a translation strategy to make this information come alive.

Now that you have identified your core content, you need to find a way to *quickly* get it into your students' heads. The next section of this book introduces numerous strategies for doing this. Right now, all you need to understand is the principle on which they are all based:

- **Engagement**—Use a translation strategy that naturally engages your students, so *all* of them pay attention and absorb the information.

Why?

If we want every student to assimilate the core information quickly, we *have* to keep their attention *all* the time. This introduces one of the most important ideas in this book: *You cannot deliver core information as a lecture* because many of your students will fail to grasp it.

If you use lecture as your primary delivery method, even dedicated students will find it hard to take in the information for more than

10 minutes. According to Jensen (2005, p. 37), "The human brain is poor at nonstop attention. It needs time for processing and rest after learning." Students who are fully engaged often take an interesting idea and mentally wander off making connections on their own, meaning they aren't listening to anything new the teacher might be saying! For less dedicated students, as most teachers have found to their cost, you will simply be giving them an opportunity to daydream, pass notes, and torment others. So don't give them the chance (Sprenger, 2009).

How?

Instead of lecturing, for this first part of the lesson, immerse your students in the learning process. Get them moving. Get them involved. Get them playing a game. Introduce elements of competition. Tell a story. Use multimedia. Create moments of self-discovery. Use lots of music. You'll find detailed explanations of all these ideas and many more in the rest of this book. For now, simply understand that you cannot lecture at this point. Later on, you can. But *not now*.

Let them talk

STEP 3 Articulate—Ensure that students have the opportunity to engage in vigorous, rigorous, and purposeful conversation about the content to increase understanding and develop ideas.

One of the quickest ways to make sure your students grasp core information quickly is to let them talk about it. At this stage, we're not looking for critical thinking, but simply for students to process the new information you've just introduced, make additional connections, and fill in any gaps.

Why?

Before they can talk about a topic, your students must first think about it. Talking is a great way to make sure this happens. As human beings talk, we verbally process the information. Talking will allow your students to come to a better understanding of the new information. They will pick up and practice using its vocabulary; take a higher level of ownership for their learning; and recognize connections between new concepts, terms, and ideas. When all of these things happen, students are more likely to understand and remember the new information.

In fact, if you don't pause frequently to let your students talk, they will find it difficult to take in all the information. As Kagan and Kagan say in their book *Kagan Cooperative Learning* (2009, p. 6.17), "Frequent processing distinguishes successful from unsuccessful teachers. Why? Working memory can only hold a limited amount of information. More information beyond about ten minutes is like pouring water into a glass that is already full." They go on to point out that if, instead of continuing to lecture, we stop at this point and let our students talk about the content, they will tag the information in their long-term memory. Then, after processing and storing the information, students can clear their working memory so they have the capacity to take in and retain new ideas (Kagan & Kagan, 2009, p. 17).

Clearly, this requires a change from traditional Red Light teaching, where the ratio of teacher to student talk has been 80:20, or even higher in favor of the teacher. This is predicated on the idea that we need to hear more from the one with the most knowledge. But perhaps we should invert that idea. If talking supports thinking, processing, understanding, and recall, then surely we need to hear more from the people with the most to *learn*.

Here's another radical idea: Giving our students the answer should be a last resort, done only after all avenues of discussion have been exhausted. We're so used to our position as "the fountain of all knowledge" that telling students the answer comes with the territory. But it shouldn't. An answer students come to as a result of their own discussions, thinking, and reasoning is an answer they both understand (by definition) and remember (because of all the processing required to get there). The amount of energy and time required to transfer information from short-term memory to long-term storage is directly related to how well they can recall it later (Jensen, 2005, p. 16).

Nigel's Notes

My nine-year-old son was struggling with math. He was still very much at the concrete stage of his mathematical workings and increasingly frustrated at not "getting it." One day my wife and I tuned in to a conversation he was having with his six-year-old sister in the car. My son was taking his sister through the rules of addition and subtraction, using examples. As the conversation went back and forth, I could almost see the lightbulbs going on in both children's heads. I wondered how much more quickly he'd have grasped the concept if he'd talked about it in class.

How?

Frequently, your translation strategy will automatically promote conversation and discussion, for example, when solving a puzzle, deciding where components should be placed on a map or diagram, or making up quiz questions. However, there will also be places where you set up conversations. This can be as simple as saying, "Turn to the person sitting next to you and find out what they think is the most likely explanation. You have one minute—go!" Or it can be far more explicit and structured.

For example:

- "In your group, come up with a series of True/False questions to test the rest of the class on this topic. You have three minutes—go!"

- "With your partner, come up with 5 to 10 questions you would like to see answered."

- "In your group, devise a question you think I could *not* answer!"

- "For each letter of the alphabet (or parts of it in groups), come up with a key word or idea related to what we have studied."

If students are not already in groups or pairs, find a quick and random means of creating them. Giving the order to "Form a group of four or five" usually dissolves into chaos and leaves unpopular students on the edges. Instead, try giving students a ticket with a symbol or number as they arrive. Then, when it's time for group discussion, their first task is to go to the part of the room where they can see the same symbol or number. Or, if you have time, ask them to find the students with the same card. This takes a bit longer but is a good brain break, usually creating laughter and lots of movement—both highly useful in keeping the human mind focused. As Kagan and Kagan (2009, p. 1.5) put it, "We can only sit so long before we become exhausted from inhibiting our impulses to move."

It's quite easy to find opportunities for students to talk, yet many teachers hesitate to put this idea into practice. Frequently, teachers feel threatened by a classroom full of talking students. We ask ourselves: "Are the students on task?" "Is my classroom too noisy?" "Am I still in control?" "Am I doing my job?" The question we're really asking is, "Will my students stay on topic?"

The short is answer is, no, of course they won't. The truth is, from time to time, most students will veer off-course during small-group discussions. But we can minimize this by

- walking around the room, listening in, asking questions, and generally guiding conversations; or

- asking groups to come up with a specific response (a question, an observation, an answer, the three most important points) they have to share with the group at the end of the discussion, providing a focus point and an incentive to participate.

However, we need to recognize that, when we first give students permission to talk, particularly if a friend is in the group, they often start off topic. "Wow, did you hear what happened on the bus this morning. . . . " This is not the moment to step in angrily. In most cases, they'll soon get it out of their system. Simply let the conversation run its course and they will return their focus to the topic at hand. If after a minute they're still off-topic, it may now be time to guide them gently back on track.

Another hurdle to implementing this part of the process is that, in many schools, a noisy class is seen as a signal that the teacher has poor classroom-management skills. If this is true of your school, you might want to preempt criticism by notifying colleagues of your new teaching strategy. Perhaps you could couch it in the following terms: "Given that the new curriculum is focusing on critical thinking, I'm trialing a different approach to lessons this term. Part of each lesson will include robust discussion and debate, so you can expect a certain level of noise from my classroom."

Whether you are struggling with your own doubts or those of others, you can take comfort in the fact that letting your students talk is a surefire learning strategy.

Help them remember . . .

STEP 4 Replicate—Deliberately build in a memory strategy to enhance recall.

While your translation strategy will embed strong recall of your core information, you also need to deliberately build in a memory strategy with each lesson. And you need to be absolutely explicit about it. In other words, there should be a moment, toward the end of the lesson, when you say: "Now, let's look at *how* we're going to remember this." Then you introduce one key memory strategy that will act as a trigger for the concept and associated detail.

Why?

Most students have no inkling of the many powerful techniques human beings can use to memorize information. Over the course of their years in education, students usually pick up a few basic memory strategies: mind maps, acronyms or acrostics, and, most frequently, repetition. However, they are only introduced to these ideas occasionally and as a side issue. Rarely does a teacher include a deliberate memory strategy as an automatic part of every lesson plan.

This begs the question: Why not? Why don't we show students how to memorize the information they need to pass the test? With practice, even less able students can successfully memorize large amounts of information easily and quickly (Allen, 2008, p. 13). Surely, making this happen should be a standard element of every lesson.

The fact that it's not comes down to a combination of factors. Some teachers still believe, erroneously, that memory strategies are for elementary students. Others have simply never seen what's possible. Until the teacher training curriculum includes a large module on this vital educational technique, memory strategies will remain sidelined. However, that's no reason why *your* students shouldn't benefit from them.

Teach your students memory strategies, and you give them the key to learning success. Once they discover they can remember lessons easily and effortlessly, they also find a new enthusiasm for learning. The positive emotions that result from discovering how easily they can remember key ideas often sparks students to engage more deeply in future lessons, and subsequently learn more, even without any additional effort on the part of the teacher (Kagan, 2000, p. 26).

How?

Some excellent books are dedicated to specific memory strategies, so we will not go into them in detail here. (For more information on these books, check the list provided at the end of this chapter.) But here are the ones you should be aware of, with some references to help you find out more about them:

- **Acronyms**—Words made out of the first letters of the key ideas to be remembered. For example, the word HOMES is often used to teach students the five Great Lakes. Acronyms help to *chunk* information so students don't have to remember a great deal of information all at once. You can make up your own, or, even better, get your students to make some up themselves.

- **Acrostics**—Series of words in which the first letters of each word form a useful word or phrase. Perhaps the best-known acrostic from music class is <u>E</u>very <u>G</u>ood <u>B</u>oy <u>D</u>oes <u>F</u>ine—representing the notes on the lines of the treble clef. Another one from math class is <u>P</u>lease <u>E</u>xcuse <u>M</u>y <u>D</u>ear <u>A</u>unt <u>S</u>ally, representing the order of operations to be done in a math problem—Parentheses, Exponents, Multiplication, Division, Addition, and Subtraction.

- **Stories**—Analogies that help students remember a concept (see Nigel's Notes for a great example) or act as mnemonic devices, where the teacher weaves the items students need to recall into a strange story. Formulas, processes that have distinct steps, and specific lists all lend themselves easily to this storytelling memory device. Simply take a series of concepts, terms, or ideas like these and link them in an unbroken, integrated sequence that creates a chain of connections. Building visual imagery into the story will make it even easier for your students to remember.

Nigel's Notes

I had a great Economics teacher at school and he enthused us even in the driest of economic theory. I distinctly remember his telling of the story of diminishing marginal returns. He didn't frame it that way; he simply related the story of a man lost in the desert for several days without a drink when out of nowhere a truck appears filled with crates of his favorite soft drink. The man devours the first can of drink in his quest to quench his thirst; his thirst is so great that a second and third can get devoured with almost equal relish. However, with each subsequent can the man's thirst is not only quenched, but he begins to feel a little off color, even sick of the thought of another of his favorite drink. We as students drank in the story, laughed at the mental picture conjured up by our storytelling teacher, and felt sick as we "drank" each further can of soft drink. At the end we were given the academic language to fit with the story, and more than 30 years later, the law of diminishing marginal returns is still alive in my brain!

- **Lyrics**—Where students write new lyrics to a well-known song using key words from a lesson. When they hum a few bars from the song, the information tumbles into their brains! (Jensen, 2001, p. 20).

- **Memory pegs**—The idea here is to learn a set of actions and images for each number 1 through 20. To *peg* an idea, students simply start with the well-known action for that number and then slightly change the action into something that will trigger a memory of the idea (Allen, 2008, p. 22). Students who learn this simple technique find, to their amazement, that they can easily recall large amounts of information. See Chapter 5 for a list of the pegs and how to teach them.

- **Mind maps**—Mind maps make excellent study notes. Get your students to include their own graphics, and put a reminder graphic in their written notes to correspond with the symbol on the map. Then, when they see the symbol, their brains will flick to the written content as well.

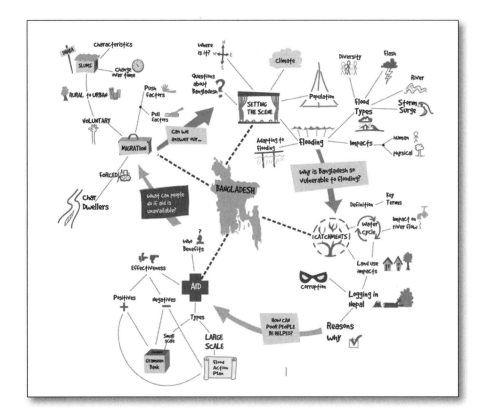

Make sure you use a variety of memory strategies. If you insist on students creating an acrostic for every lesson, they'll quickly become bored. Mix it up and try to match content against a bank of strategies at your disposal.

Checking in to Gauge Memory Strategy Effectiveness

Once you start using memory strategies, it's important to check that they are actually working. Here are some ideas for quickly assessing student understanding, either at the end of the lesson you've just taught (Exit Checks) or at the beginning of the next one (Entry Checks).

Exit Checks

- **Brain Check 1**—Place a chart on the wall next to the door with the concepts as titles to the appropriate number of columns. As they leave, ask students to score their understanding of each in each column/concept, 1 being "I really got it" and 5 being "What was that all about?"

- **Brain Check 2**—Rather than gauge each concept individually (as described above), ask students to rank each concept from 1, the "best understood," and then in ascending order to the least understood.

- **One thing before you go**—For a more informal check, stand at the door and state, "No one leaves until they tell me something they have learned today!" Students enjoy the humor behind this and clamor to tell the teacher something of importance as they leave.

- **Tick or Cross**—Provide each student with two slips of paper about five minutes before the end of the lesson, one slip with a green tick on the left side and the other with a red cross on the left side. On the green-tick slip, students write in what they have really understood over recent lessons in sentence or point form, while on the red-cross slip, they itemize the concepts they do not yet quite understand. Next lesson, use the results of your check to set the context for what you're about to cover. For example, you could say, "I went through your ticks and crosses last night, and I obviously need to go over . . . " or "As a class you ranked . . . concept as the least understood, so today we will revisit it and try to improve everyone's understanding."

Entry Checks

- **Speed test**—Give groups of students a piece of flip chart paper with the key vocabulary words from the previous lesson. Challenge them to come up with definitions for or examples of these concepts as quickly as possible.

- **Picture me**—If the previous lesson contained a key diagram, challenge groups of students to reproduce it on a piece of flip chart paper. After 1 minute, allow "cheating" where students have 20 seconds to run around the room and "steal" other people's ideas. After 3 minutes, put all the charts up on the wall, and decide which team got closest to the correct version.

Entry and Exit Checks are good instruments of formative assessment, offering insights into what worked and what didn't, so the lesson can be improved next time. They also serve as useful bridges across lessons, helping to preserve the continuum of learning as well as helping students to make the connections between lessons.

Encourage critical thinking . . .

STEP 5   **Criticate**—Plan strategies for encouraging critical thinking.

To criticate is not a verb, but perhaps it should be! Once your students know and understand the core information, they are in a position to start thinking about it—critically. This means, as set out in Chapter 1, we need to get our students

- understanding the logical relationships between ideas;
- assessing, appraising, and evaluating various lines of reasoning;
- detecting inconsistencies, mistakes, and errors in arguments;
- identifying the relevance and importance of ideas; and
- reflecting on their own beliefs, principals, standards, and values.

We want our students to apply and extend their understanding in other contexts and to develop a deeper understanding of the concept (Costa, 2008).

Nigel's Notes

I remember my older brother's advice when as a young boy I was studying earnestly for an exam, parrot learning all the information. He said, "You're trying too hard. Just try to understand what you're studying and you'll remember it." While he didn't call it critical thinking, that's what he meant. Eventually, I stopped learning things by rote and instead started finding out how and why they worked. To my astonishment, I found it easy to remember the facts I'd previously spent hours trying to remember.

Why?

As critical thinking is an increasing part of the curriculum, the most obvious answer to this question is: Because you need it for the test! However, there are higher educational reasons for encouraging critical thinking, which are explained brilliantly on a website created by the Department of Philosophy at the University of Hong Kong: http://philosophy.hku.hk/think/critical/ct.php. On the site, Dr. Joe Lau and Dr. Jonathan Chan answer the question "Why study critical thinking?" With kind permission, their eloquent response is reproduced below.

- **Critical thinking is a domain-general thinking skill**. The ability to think clearly and rationally is important whatever we choose to do. If you work in education, research, finance, management or the legal profession, then critical thinking is obviously important. But critical thinking skills are not restricted to a particular subject area. Being able to think well and solve problems systematically is an asset for any career.

- **Critical thinking is very important in the new knowledge economy**. The global knowledge economy is driven by information and technology. One has to be able to deal with changes quickly and effectively. The new economy places increasing demands on flexible intellectual skills, and the ability to analyze information and integrate diverse sources of knowledge in solving problems. Good critical thinking promotes such thinking skills, and is very important in the fast-changing workplace.

- **Critical thinking enhances language and presentation skills**. Thinking clearly and systematically can improve the way we express our ideas. In learning how to analyze the logical structure of texts, critical thinking also improves comprehension abilities.

- **Critical thinking promotes creativity**. To come up with a creative solution to a problem involves not just having new ideas. It must also be the case that the new ideas being generated are useful and relevant to the task at hand. Critical thinking plays a crucial role in evaluating new ideas, selecting the best ones, and modifying them if necessary.

- **Critical thinking is crucial for self-reflection**. To live a meaningful life and to structure our lives accordingly, we need to justify and reflect on our values and decisions. Critical thinking provides the tools for this process of self-evaluation.

How?

Most critical thinking takes place toward the end of a unit of study or at the culmination of a particular task. Lower order thinking has taken place earlier in the process; now it's time for you to guide your students toward a higher order level of analysis by using the following strategies:

- **Teacher modeling**—According to Epstein (2008, p. 42), "To help children become creative thinkers and problem solvers, teachers must exercise critical thinking themselves." So, share your own thought processes with your students—literally, talk them through your thinking as you try to solve a problem. For visual learners, support this by *unpacking* your thoughts on the board in a flow diagram. Reflect out loud about how the content relates to a real-world situation or to your own values; voice your concerns about a potential flaw in or limitation of an idea; or talk about why you believe this information is more (or less) important than the material you discussed last week. After a few weeks, whenever students give an answer, prompt them to share their thinking with the class. This should become the default response mode in your classroom. Rather than

"The answer is . . . ," you should expect

"The answer is . . . because . . . however, if . . . "

- **Questions from you**—Pose team questions that make your students think about and discuss the content. Avoid questions with yes/no answers.

Purpose of Your Questions	Example Questions
Encourage students to think about how the ideas might connect to other learning	• Where else have you seen this pattern? • What is this an example of? • What does this remind you of?
Prompt students to come up with a line of reasoning	• Why would someone choose to act this way? • What would happen if? • Why did this happen?
Encourage students to find errors in an argument or seek substantiation of a belief	• When wouldn't this be true? • Does this idea always hold true? • What makes you think this is true? • What if this factor changed? Would it still be true?
Help students to understand how the idea relates to the real world or might be important	• How could you use this idea to solve a problem in your own life? • In what careers might you need to understand this concept? • When would understanding this concept save your life/make you rich?
Encourage students to make value judgments about the new information	• Do you agree with this idea? • Why/why not? • What would you do if . . . ?

- **Questions from them**—Ask your students to develop thoughtful questions about the topic beyond the factual or simplistic. Again, modeling is required. Get them to think about "What if?" questions. This is a great opportunity for collaboration within groups where the meeting of minds not only aids a deeper understanding but helps to develop thinking. Once students have developed their own questions, they can challenge other groups to answer them, or you can use them to lead a whole group discussion.

- **New context**—Applying the concept in another context will certainly test their depth of understanding. At the start of the next lesson, set up a simulation that requires students to apply their knowledge.

- **Newsroom**—Ask your students to act as a newspaper team to create stories about the content covered. Assign stories to each team, requiring them to think about and research the core content. Each team will need to appoint an editor, researchers, writers, and a layout designer (responsible for headlines and visuals). You act as the managing editor, reminding them of deadlines and approving content. At the end of the process, students can vote for the best newspaper produced.

- **Video thinking**—Video clips or whole documentaries offer great potential to prompt critical thinking. Here are some options:
  - Show the video once, with the setup that there will be questions afterward. Then give students or teams the questions and challenge them to see how many questions they can answer. Next, show the video again for them to fill in the gaps.
  - Show the video once and get the teams to come up with questions for other teams to answer. Repeat the two-stage process above.
  - Show the video in sections, posing "What happens next?" questions before revealing the next segment.
  - Use the video as a research resource, where students self-regulate its viewing, stopping and starting it until they have discovered the answers or made their decisions.

- **Lights, camera, action**—Use an online forum to allow small groups of students to plan, storyboard, write, direct, edit, film, and present short documentary-style films on the topic being studied.

Over time, your students will begin to recognize the difference between lower and higher order thinking. This will open up avenues for students to apply and extend their understanding, ultimately leading to them "cutting the apron strings" attached to the teacher.

How Green Light Strategies Align With the Process

Green Light Strategies		High School Application	
Connections	Creating a hook on which students can hang new information	ISOLATE	
Movement	Physically engaging students in the learning process	**Games**	T R A N S L A T E
Drama	Theatrics, story-telling, and students acting out the learning	**Stories**	
Novelty	Harnessing something *different* to capture students' attention	**Props** **New technology**	
Socialization	Student-to-student discussions, processing, and debriefs	ARTICULATE	
Memory **Visuals**	Pegs, association, acrostics, and rhyming Posters, mind maps, doodles, and drawing	REPLICATE	
Tone	Music	DELIVERY	
Emotion	Laughter, curiosity, and anticipation		

USEFUL BOOKS ABOUT MEMORY
AND MEMORY STRATEGIES

The Complete Idiot's Guide to Improving Your Memory. Michael Kurland & Richard Lupoff. Alpha Book, 1999.

Don't Forget. Danielle Lapp. Addison-Wesley, 1987.

The Great Memory Book. Karen Markowitz & Eric Jensen. Corwin, 1999.

Improving Your Memory. Richard McAndler. Gill & MacMilliam, Ltd., 2002.

Kevin Trudeau's Mega Memory. Kevin Trudeau. William Morrow, 1995.

Memory. Elizabeth Loftus. Addison-Wesley, 1980.

Remember Everything You Read. Stanley D. Frank, Ed.D. Random House, 1990.

Total Memory Workout: 8 Easy Steps to Maximum Memory Fitness. Cynthia R. Green, Ph.D. Bantam, 1999.

Use Your Perfect Memory. Tony Buzan. Penguin Books, 1990.

Your Memory. Kenneth L. Higbee, Ph.D. Marlowe & Company, 2001.

3

Translation Techniques

Without proper translation, all teaching is lost.

Translating core content into an engaging activity is the key to holding students' attention during this critical stage of the learning process. However, during the course of the year, try to use as many and as varied translation techniques as you can. Each topic might need a different translation strategy. If you use the same one over and over, your lessons will become predictable and fail to spark student curiosity. You will also run the risk of students getting current content mixed up with content they learned previously using the same activity.

Gaming Strategies

"Human beings are typically interested in puzzles and games even though they may be of little consequence in terms of long-term goals or deeply held values; witness the number of people who do crossword puzzles and play video games in their leisure time."

(Marzano, 2007, p. 101)

Why We Need to Get Serious About Making Learning Fun

For many high school teachers, the very word *game* sets off alarm bells. After all, if our students are playing a game, how can they take our lesson seriously? This is not elementary school. Surely we no longer have to baby our students by making learning fun?

In fact, not only is it OK to make high school learning fun, it is actually far more efficient and effective. When students have fun with a game, they are in almost the perfect state for accelerated learning: engaged, motivated, and swirling with the positive emotions that not only encourage logical thinking and processing but also lay down strong memories.

By design, games ensure 100% participation and interaction. They effortlessly tap into natural learning strategies, such as competition and cooperation, and they have built-in momentum. Make any activity a game and see how much faster it gets done. No matter how dull the task, inject a little competition, and watch how motivated even the most sophisticated high school senior becomes.

Also, if your students learn core content while playing a game, they will have much stronger memories of it, for three reasons. First, games have structures that your students are extremely familiar with, creating a natural hook on which to hang the new information in your core content. Second, they will learn this content as a process of discovery, creating deeper understanding than if you simply told them the information. Third, the emotions they experience during the game (curiosity, anticipation) are "appetitive" states that stimulate the mental appetite (Jensen, 2005), helping to construct deeper memories that are easy to access. Kagan (2000, p. 26) explains this further: "When there is emotion, the neurons in the brain actually fire at an increased level signaling the hippocampus that this stimuli is worth remembering."

In addition, many teachers love using games because it changes their role in the classroom; they move out of the spotlight as "font of all knowledge and person responsible for learning" and instead end up on the sidelines as umpire and coach. This requires less energy on the part of the teacher and puts the responsibility for learning in the hands of the students—the key to educational engagement.

Finally, games offer a simple means of getting high school students to collaborate without drama. The combination of hormones, teen angst, and the dread of being uncool renders most teenagers socially inept. Nothing is more likely to put the kiss of death on a lesson than starting it with the immortal words "We're going to do some group work today!" But throw your students into a game and they will collaborate automatically, without realizing they are— horror of horrors!—engaging with their peers in a spirit of cooperation.

Where to Find Inspiration

You can use any game your students are familiar with, but here are a few universally popular structures to get you started.

Sports

You can either actually replicate popular sporting formats in the classroom or harness elements of sporting culture. Replicating a format means coming up with a classroom version of scoring a point or making a goal. For example, for tennis, players *hit* the ball back by answering a question correctly. Get it wrong and the other player wins the point. You can set this up on a whole class level, with half the class on each side, chairs facing each other. Add a layer of drama by letting the teams choose a famous player to represent and throwing a giant tennis ball to the team answering the question.

Alternatively, simply harness the sporting context: put your students in teams; put them against the clock; announce a prize for the first to finish; or stand on a desk and commentate. All of these setups create a different dynamic in your classroom—they help to make learning fun.

Board Games

Many subjects already have published versions of board games to teach core content. Some were created decades ago, such as the Development Spiral Game.[1] You'll find more modern games for most subjects at http://thefunwaytolearn.com. Excellent online game generators also exist (try www.teach-nology.com), where you can plug in key vocabulary or concepts to create popular games, such as bingo, for the whole class.

Alternatively, you can cut out cost and advance preparation by allowing your students to make their own games. One of the most popular weeks of the year in Nigel's department is when 200 Year 9 geography students spend a week creating their own board games based on the year's core content. This collaborative epic culminates in the final day, when the students play each other's games. The result is an astonishingly rich learning experience, with 100% participation and engagement, which becomes the ultimate form of review. Students' recall of the material they studied in order to create and play the games is always extremely high.

Jigsaws

Jigsaws lend themselves to self-discovery. They are ideal when students need to remember models, processes, graph shapes, constituent parts, or the way ideas fit together. You can use them by

- cutting up a picture of the model or diagram and challenging teams to race each other to reassemble the picture;
- mixing up the real pieces with unrelated content, so the puzzle can only be put together if your students figure out which bits to use;

---

[1]Originally published in *The South*, Punnett & Webber, Blackwell Education, 1989; ISBN 0-631-90148-5.

- laminating larger sheets and asking students to come up in front of the class and put them in the right place inside a framework drawn on your board;

- handing out parts of a process or timeline and asking a student or a team to place them on the floor in the correct order—with the person doing the placing justifying why they positioned their piece in that way;

- deliberately leaving out a critical piece and asking students to create the missing element themselves.

Tips for Creating Jigsaws

- They can apply to everything—even an essay can be a jigsaw when you ask students to put paragraphs in the right order.

- Don't make them too hard—you want students to get to the answer fairly quickly.

- If some people are struggling, allow "cheating"—give teams 1 minute to go and look at what other people are doing and "steal" their ideas.

- Color code the pieces so at a glance you can see if your students are on the right track and gauge the time until completion.

- You don't have to create identical jigsaws; cut things up differently if you want to stop blatant cheating.

Television

Almost from the moment television broadcasting began in the 1940s, game shows and reality TV have drawn massive viewing audiences. From the popularity of *Candid Camera* (1940s) and *Jeopardy* (1960s) through to the modern-day record ratings of *Who Wants to Be a Millionaire?* and *Survivor*, people of all ages continue to tune in—by the millions.

For today's high school students, the rules and structures of these shows are familiar, compelling, and highly engaging. In fact, they are almost scientifically designed to deliver the right combination of fascination, suspense, and gratification to keep audiences coming back for more. TV production companies spend vast resources researching, pilot testing, and refining each format before going into full production. Rather than reinventing the wheel, we can harness these proven (and paid for!) engagement vehicles in the classroom to great effect.

Used appropriately, a TV game show formula will grab the attention of every student—whether participating or watching—with learning becoming almost a side effect of their participation and engagement.

Tips for Using TV Formats

- Listen in—find out what shows your students are currently watching. If classroom conversation doesn't yield this information, take a popularity poll.

- Choose formats with both collaboration *and* competition—look for shows where
  o People work in teams
  o Competition underpins each task
  o People compete for an ultimate prize
  o There are clear rules
  o Time limits sometimes apply (for example, *Survivor* and *The Amazing Race* tick all the boxes for creating a classroom environment charged with energy and excitement)

- Avoid games that rely on elimination; while drawing terrific ratings, people being voted out and other ritual humiliations are unhelpful in the context of learning. In the classroom, you want to keep everyone engaged and participating throughout the game.

- Use the theme tune; TV formats come with a sound track. Play their iconic theme tunes in the background as students complete each activity.

How to Adapt Games for Use in Your Classroom

The key to making any game work as a learning tool is to link the outcome of the game or puzzle to the core idea your students are going to investigate. The link with this content and the fun of the game must be clear, strong, and absolutely unambiguous. Strangely, although students love games, if they can't see the learning value in the result, they will quickly disengage. This does not mean you have to explain why you're doing this activity upfront. Some content does need a big framing session for the lesson to make sense. At other times, you can set up intrigue by simply throwing students into the game and then debriefing them by asking, "Why did we just do that?" Unlabelled games like this can result in powerful learning, as students' curiosity is piqued, keeping their attention until they figure out what's going on.

Make sure your students can complete the game in a reasonable time. The game should not take over the lesson; it's a means to an end. In general, spend no more than 10 to 15 minutes on the game itself. This is usually sufficient time to get the point across. Then you can move along and do the thinking. Try to get your students onto the next task as quickly as possible. At the conclusion of the game, they will be mentally ready for the next stage of learning.

Many games are more effective if they include a token prize. The prize must be minor, but still worth winning. Candy is always popular. Or you might use an over-the-top trophy that sits with the victorious team until the end of the lesson, and then is given back. Or the prize could be the rest of the class performing a "we're not worthy" bow to the winners. The key is to find something that works with your students.

Finally, be aware that introducing a game increases the amount of movement and noise in your classroom, so you may need to use different classroom-management techniques. The following strategies will help to stop purposeful activity from dissolving into chaos.

Set the Guidelines

Right up front, establish some basic ground rules—and not just the rules of the game. Make sure you head off potential objections and interruptions with something along the lines of this: "I am the umpire and my decision is final." You can steer students to both behave and make progress with ongoing commentary, but make sure you keep your commentary light. You want to create a low level of competition, but nothing particularly serious. Respond to complaints in a light-hearted manner. For example,

"But why don't we have as many people as they do?"

"Because you have superior brain power on your side . . . "

or . . .

"But we had to go first last time!"

"That's because you're lucky and special . . . "

Command the Room as the Umpire

It's harder to get the attention of the class during a game, so use different tactics: jump on a desk; use music to control the crowd (see Chapter 5); and make sure students physically turn and look at you before you give them an instruction.

Give Clear Instructions (Allen, 2010)

- Be clear and concise—Use as few words as possible to convey the *essence* of the communication.

  Rather than: *Now I want you to figure out which is the first piece.*

  Use instead: *Find the first piece—go!*

  If we stick to what is essential, students are more likely to hear, understand, and do what they're asked.

- Give directions *one at a time*—Give your students one direction, and then wait until it has been completed before moving to the next one.

- Use a step check whenever possible—Check to make sure every student, or team, has completed each direction before you give the next one.

- Be congruent—Make three elements congruent when giving instructions.

  1. Make sure your tone of voice supports the fact that you are giving directions; don't shout, but be authoritative.

  2. Use hand gestures to add clarity—demonstrate the circle you're asking your students to make; hold up fingers to reinforce numbers; point in the direction you want them to move; and so on.

  3. Use body language to further emphasize the idea—turn your body in the direction they must go to get a handout; lean to one side if they must lean over to talk to another student; walk toward the door if everyone is heading to another room.

- Use the Four Part Sequence—This is a four-part framework for directions that helps students to complete the instruction successfully.

	Intent	Example
1	Establish a time frame for the students to act on the direction	*"In 10 seconds . . . "*
2	Embed a trigger to signal the start of that movement	*"When I say go . . . "*
3	Give the directions clearly and concisely	*"Move the chairs to the sides of the room."*
4	Pull the trigger	*"Go."*

Story-Telling

"There have been great societies that did not use the wheel, but there have been no societies that did not tell stories."

—Ursula K. Le Guin (storyteller.net)

Why We're Never Too Old for Story Time

Story-telling is one of the oldest forms of instruction. For centuries, it was the only means human beings had for passing on important information to the next generation. Even today in our digital age, spoken stories remain the primary vehicle for teaching young children about the world. Yet, perhaps because we associate stories with childhood, we often stop using them as a regular instruction method in high schools.

This is a mistake. Whether we are adults or children, stories have unique qualities we can harness to support the learning process. Stories are natural to the way our brains think about and process information. Their structure and sequence make them instantly engaging and extremely easy to remember.

Tulving (1984) coined the phrase "episodic memory" to describe the part of our long-term memory that is particularly tuned to narrative. This is why we find it much easier to remember ideas we receive in the form of a story than, say, those we receive in the form of a list.

Stories are also inherently compelling because they are full of moments of interest. "What happens next?" "Why did he do that?" "How is that possible?" are all effortlessly engaging questions that stories raise constantly with an audience.

Even poor story-tellers hold their audience's attention far, far longer than those reading data off of PowerPoint slides—where most people tune out after a couple of minutes. If you're narrating a story, the question "Why are you telling me this?" will keep listeners engaged for an astonishingly long time. Consider that time you were trapped by someone at a social event, who insisted on telling you a long, involved, and ultimately uninteresting story. Yet, how long did you pay attention in the vain hope that "surely this is going somewhere"? And how much of the story could you remember the next day? The story you tell your students doesn't have to be particularly exciting; its structure will hold their attention and make its content easily memorable.

Stories are also extremely useful as the foundation for critical thinking because they show how ideas interact. They also offer opportunities for students to consider "What would happen if?" and have embedded values. You can ask your students to critically deconstruct a story—to great learning effect.

Where to Find Inspiration

We come across hundreds of stories every day, from our conversations with family and friends, from the news, and from our own experiences and observations. We just need to have our antennas up to recognize everyday stories for the potential they provide. You may not see the link between core content and what you saw, heard, or talked about until months later. So, tuck every story away for future reference. Here are some of the richest places to mine for story gold:

My Life–Your Life

Students are fascinated by personal anecdotes. Use experiences from your own life or those of family, friends, or acquaintances. Stories about disaster, human error, or illogical behavior are always popular. For example, an economics teacher always begins his unit on brand loyalty with a true story about Greg the builder who is passionate about the Apple brand. As they hear how Greg spends all of his money buying up each new iPod, iPad, and iPhone, the students do the math, with audible gasps. With a 2-minute story, the point is made and is never to be forgotten—brand value translates into big dollars and potentially irrational purchasing behavior.

Travel

Traveling offers many opportunities to grow your story bank, and not just from your own experiences. From taxi and bus drivers, to wait staff and shopkeepers, the characters you meet all have a story to tell, so collect them!

News

Nothing says relevant like last night's news story. If your students heard the item, then so much the better, as they already have a hook on which to hang the new information you are going to tie to the story. If they didn't, you are plugging a gap in their knowledge of current affairs. News stories are particularly good translation techniques because of the potential for constant review: Every time your students hear the story on the TV or radio, they will be prompted to recall your content.

Peers

Students place more significance on stories about people they know. Ask permission to share your colleagues' experiences. *"Did you know that Mr. Smith . . . "* or *"I was talking to Mrs. Jones the other day and she told me this incredible story . . . "*

Fantasy

Sometimes, it's worth spending time making up a story to fit the facts of the core content you are introducing. In this way, you are constructing a memory device. If your students can remember the story, they can also remember the content. (See, for example, in Chapter 4, Geography lesson #4—Relief Maps.)

As a humorous but important side note, feel free to expand the story in any direction necessary to make sure you've communicated the key point. Don't get trapped by the need to adhere to the truth. As the old saying goes,

The Number One Rule of Teaching:

Never let the truth *get in the way of a good story!*

How to Adapt Stories in the Classroom

As with a game, your story must have a direct and strong link with your core content. Don't tell a story unless you plan to reference it as a memory hook, recall device, or jumping-off point for critical thinking. Keep it short, and take out any irrelevant subplots that don't support the core idea you are conveying.

Stories are inherently engaging, but the following strategies will help you strengthen their impact:

Create a Relaxed Atmosphere

Don't expect or allow students to take notes while you're telling a story. They will actually record much stronger memories if you let them sit back and take it in. You probably need to say, "*Sit back and relax. I only want you to listen.*" Many teachers feel guilty when they indulge in stories because they are easy to tell and popular with students, who appear to get a break from "real" schoolwork. Nothing could be further from the truth. Used appropriately, stories are powerful learning tools.

Timing

Although stories are excellent translation strategies to connect your students with core content at the beginning of your lesson, you can also use them in other places to create different effects. Perhaps a story could be a useful segue into the critical thinking stage, offering a scenario for students to consider or discuss. Or it might be the final piece of powerful learning in the high-attention moments at the end of the lesson, when student engagement soars with the prospect of the bell. Tell a story that synthesizes the ideas you have just taught, and your students will take away strong and positive memories of the lesson.

Technique

Make your storytelling technique match the story. For a quick, personal anecdote to connect students with the content, use the "fireside chat" approach, where you might sit on a desk and relay the story informally. However, if your story is the core memory strategy, you can support student understanding and recall with large, congruent gestures. For example, if your hero climbs a mountain, stand on a chair when he reaches the summit; if the waves get bigger, demonstrate with your hands; if possible, mime the actions—open the door, point to the man on the cliff; if there's a shocking moment, jump back yourself. You'll find that adding "pictures" to your story in this way will greatly improve recall when you ask students to retell the tale; in fact, you'll probably see them mirroring your gestures as they try to recall the story. You might want to test this theory out for yourself: Deliberately underscore one idea with gestures and leave another unsupported—which fact did your students remember best?

Set the Stage

If your story is at the beginning of the lesson, you can build on the previous idea with a little stage setting before your students arrive. This may include appropriate background music, different lighting, props, or even costumes. You might also put up posters or photographs as scenery, or move the furniture to help set the stage. For example, create a corridor down the middle of the classroom to walk up and down. All of this creates a sense of anticipation in your classroom, making students highly receptive to learning.

Guests

You don't have to be the story-teller. If your school has visiting guests, find out if they have stories relevant to your syllabus. For example, in Sydney, Australia, a group of visiting Aboriginal elders kindly shared their life experiences with students studying the way traditional people manage ecosystems. Hearing their real life stories was far more powerful for students than reading the same information in a textbook.

Propping Up the Learning

"A pun is the lowest form of humor, unless you thought of it yourself."

—Doug Larson

How Props Help to Create Memories

Props are one of the easiest ways of connecting the topic with your students' world. Introducing a familiar object as the focus for your lesson has two benefits: one neurological and one psychological. First, it begins the process of embedding a strong memory (Garner, 2007, p. 37). Schema theory tells us that students can remember a surprisingly large amount of information *if* they can cluster it with related existing ideas. This is why it's important for teachers to remind students of previously learned information if today's topic connects with it. But what if some of your students don't have a strong memory of the previous information, or what if this is an entirely new topic?

If you can establish the starting point of a strong connection with something they are extremely familiar with, your students will have an anchor around which to tether the subsequent information. Not only that, but you will have aroused their curiosity. This is the second benefit, and a bone of contention for many high school teachers. There is a school of thought that believes it's not a teacher's job to engender curiosity in his or her students. The argument goes something like this: By the time kids reach high school, we should no longer have to baby them through the learning process. They're old enough to sit still, knuckle down, and get on with it.

Regardless of your position in this debate, there's a fairly compelling rationale for sparking student curiosity: An interested student is so much easier to teach! (Jensen, 2005, p. 77; Kirsch, 1999, p. 7; Marzano, 2007, p. 101). If we can get our students hooked early on, they are more likely to be engaged and pay attention for the duration of the lesson.

Where to Find Inspiration

When it comes to finding a prop to create a connection, you don't have to come up with a perfect analogy that works for the entire lesson. The connection with your chosen prop might only appear for a minute at the beginning of the lesson. When you review the core information, sometimes the connection virtually jumps off the page. This is ideal, because it suggests a strong and obvious link. That said, the connection doesn't have to be direct or even particularly good. Tenuous or corny connections create laughter, which is an excellent learning tool in its own right. So, if inspiration doesn't strike you right away, don't give up on the possibility of using a prop. Here are some ideas to try:

Google

Search the Internet for your core concept words, and follow links familiar to your students. Try searching images as well. For example, Googling "reverse osmosis" gives you "water filters." Googling images for "filter" gives you coffee filters. Coffee could be your connection.

Key Words

Quite often the connection is in the words you'd use to explain the key concept. For example, in economics, the topic of Aid to Developing nations covers the historical practice of the World Bank to encourage recipients to target cash crops rather than self-sufficiency, thus leading to a Band-Aid solution. In this case, the teacher opened the class by giving a Band-Aid to every student, which they stuck in their notes! Similarly, a lesson introducing the ecosystem acronym BELL (see page 19) began with the teacher walking up and down ringing a handbell.

Think Laterally

Can you use a prop that demonstrates the key idea? For example, to set up a discussion on why it's important for models to be accurate, a teacher asked each student to make a paper plane. They quickly discovered the model planes that flew the farthest were those built closest to real-world specifications. Similarly, to open a lesson on salinity, the teacher offered students a drink of salty water. The horrified spluttering quickly transitioned into a robust discussion about the effect of salinity on flora and fauna.

Nigel's Notes

I use an old paint tin and a brush as the connection prop when I teach the concept of bioaccumulation, which refers to how pollutants enter a food chain. Why the tin and brush? Paint is a common pollutant. Here's how I use the props: as my students arrive, I wander around the class brushing away at various surfaces, including their desks and walls. As I go, I make terrible jokes such as, "I think you need to brush up on this" or "I want to paint you a picture of . . ." After a few minutes, the students are desperate to know what I'm going on about. Now I can explain, and when they finally get it, groans ring out across the classroom—but now I've got their attention, and they're interested!

How to Use Props in the Classroom

Generally, props appear at the beginning of a lesson to create a memory hook. But you can also use multiple props sequentially throughout your lesson to act as memory building blocks. Here are some tips to help prop up the learning in your classroom:

One or Many

You can choose to have a single prop, for your own use, temporarily give one to each team, or provide one for each student to stick beside his or her work as a memory trigger. Although this last option can be very effective, it may also be prohibitively expensive. Don't feel you have to go this route; you can use a single prop from home at zero cost to great effect.

Complement

Props can sometimes work throughout your opening activity, but they often merely support or introduce other translation strategies. For example, a giant tennis ball tossed around the room might segue into your tennis quiz. Even if it is just your opener, don't discount the power of a prop to help anchor a memory.

Packaging

You don't have to use a prop directly; it can just be the packaging for an activity. For example, the topic of recycling lends itself to having team activity materials packaged in a plastic supermarket bag.

Review

Bring the prop back on the day of review to trigger memories, or place several around the room during a test.

Furniture

Desks and chairs can themselves serve as props. Use them to build a circle pattern in the room to represent a global or circular concept being studied.

People as Props

Occasionally, a fellow staff member can serve as your prop. He or she might have a direct link to the subject matter being studied (for example, a Vietnam veteran can enhance a history lesson) or might simply be there as your "straight" man, asking questions that open up a discussion.

Technology

"Any sufficiently advanced technology is indistinguishable from magic."

—Arthur C. Clarke (1973, p. 14)

iUse, iLearn, iRemember

Teenagers and today's technology are the perfect storm of nanosecond attention spans and instant gratification. Many high school students wear technology like a second skin, whether as the ultimate accessory, the lifeline out of hell, or the only bright spot of entertainment in an otherwise boring school day. Clearly, if we can bring any of technology's glamour, comfort, or excitement into our classrooms, engagement levels will soar, at least temporarily.

Of course, doing so is expensive and fraught with pitfalls. Although half of your class may have iPhones sitting in their school bags, you cannot use them in your classroom. As teachers, our duty of care requires technology to be approved, restricted, and controlled. So, unless you have unlimited resources, technology is unlikely to be a regular translation strategy in your classroom.

That said, many schools are rapidly embracing approved technology, and, as the price comes down, we can expect interactive whiteboards, digital cameras, and computers to become increasingly common across the teaching landscape. The point is, you certainly don't need technology to teach effectively, but anytime you get the chance to include it as an integral part of your teaching practice, you should take the opportunity to do so.

If you are lucky enough to have access to learning technologies, the key is to use them *deliberately* to support the learning process. Like any other learning tool, technology is only as good as the teacher who wields it. No matter how bright and shiny it may appear, technology per se is not enough to keep your students' attention, improve understanding, or embed memories. Teachers can be just as boring or ineffective in PowerPoint or using an interactive whiteboard as they were when writing on the blackboard—and arguably more so, given the potential for cluttered slides, confusing charts, and distracting features.

In fact, as Marzano's 2009 study suggested, teachers who don't understand how to integrate technology appropriately into their teaching can get *worse* results. The study, which involved 85 teachers and 170 classrooms, tracked teachers using interactive whiteboards to teach a set of lessons, which they then taught to a different group of students without the technology (Marzano & Haystead, 2009). In general, the study indicated that using interactive whiteboards was associated with a 16-percentage-point gain in student achievement. However, in 23% of cases, teachers had better results *without* the interactive whiteboards.

When Marzano and his team reviewed the videotapes of these teachers as compared with teachers whose results had improved with the whiteboards, they identified several marked differences in how the teachers were using the technology. For example, one of the great features of an interactive whiteboard is the voting device. This is a handheld device that enables every student to respond to questions, with the percentage of correct answers immediately displayed on the board. From a Green Light perspective, the device offers multiple advantages: an emotionally safe way for every student to participate; an instant assessment of the class's general level of understanding; a reason to set up student discussions before voting; a jumping-off point to discuss the merits of one answer versus another one; and an opportunity to discover the thinking that went into the correct answer.

However, Marzano discovered that the teachers whose results got worse weren't doing any of this; they were merely using the device, noting the number of students who got the right answer, and moving on; whereas the successful teachers integrated the voting device into a broader exploration of the content. Similarly, when teachers who had worse results with the technology used the virtual applause feature to signal a correct answer, their emphasis was on eliciting the applause rather than on clarifying the content. Just like any other translation strategy, technology can be distracting if "used without a clear focus on essential content" (Marzano, 2009, p. 82). This is why we take the trouble to *isolate* our core content before developing our teaching strategy.

How to Use Technology in the Classroom

Let us start with the, we hope, obvious point that it is not enough to put an interactive whiteboard (or any other technology) in the classroom—schools must also invest in teaching educators how to use these tools effectively. Many excellent professional development courses are designed to show teachers how to incorporate specific types of technology into their teaching practice, and this book does not intend to replicate their content. However, here are some general principles for using technology to support the learning process:

Remember Your Purpose

Everything we do in the classroom should have a purpose: to help students to engage with, understand, learn, think about, and remember content. This applies equally to technology. Just because you can think of an application for technology doesn't mean you should use it. Ask yourself: Why am I using this tool? How does it support the learning process? Why is this better than an alternative strategy?

For example, a math teacher sends out students to find real-world examples of obtuse and acute angles around the school. The students sketch the angles they find, label their location, and bring their drawings back for the class to look at. When this teacher was first given some digital cameras, he thought he would upgrade his lesson by getting students to take photographs instead. But he discovered the technology got in the way of the lesson: it took too long for every group to download and print their photographs. He returned to the traditional method, which also had the benefit of getting students to practice drawing the angles.

Integrate and Enhance

Technology is not the lesson (unless you're teaching computer studies). Use it to enhance your natural teaching practice, not take it over. For example, an English teacher has always asked to students to act out Shakespeare's sonnets. She assigns one couplet per student, with participants standing in a row and acting out the complete sonnet to great hilarity. Now, she videos these skits and replays them on her interactive whiteboard as the introduction to her review sessions. Her strategy hasn't changed, but the technology creates a richer learning experience for her students.

Mix It Up

Don't be constrained if you only have one computer or one camera. You can use technology as a reward or simply as an alternative option. For example, if students are researching answers at different stations, one station could have the class computer while the others have different textbooks. As long as students rotate every few minutes, everyone will get their technology fix. Alternatively, the math teacher mentioned previously sometimes rewards the student or team first to finish in a previous activity with use of the digital camera while the rest of the students have to draw their angles by hand.

Pace the Content

Technology offers us the possibility to present our students with a far richer range of visuals, from YouTube clips, to website images, to eye-catching graphics. These are excellent learning support tools, but be sure to give your students sufficient time to take in, analyze, and think about the content. In particular, when you put up a new chart, pause and wait for your students to assimilate the new information before starting to explain it. After you've played a video, set up small-group discussions to prompt students to process its content.

Keep Graphics Simple

It's easy to confuse students with complex digital flipchart pages or PowerPoint slides. Focus on the core content and, again, make sure visuals are there for a reason. Before you start designing charts, group your information into manageable segments and decide how you can use visuals to support the learning process. As a general rule, avoid too many visuals per slide and keep text to a minimum. In addition, avoid templates, as they add unnecessary images to the screen. Adhere to the basic rule of *clean the screen!*

4

Demonstration Lessons

Putting It All Together

Now let's look at how to assemble the previous pieces into a comprehensive lesson format. What follows are a series of lessons developed using the basic five-part process from Chapter 2.

Isolate, Translate, Articulate, Replicate, and Criticate

Remember, this is the *process* for designing your lesson; it is not always the order of the lesson plan. The lesson format will become apparent as you look through the following demonstration lessons. Note that each lesson comes with suggestions for room setup and sound track. You'll find more about these ideas in Chapter 5.

MATHEMATICS

Lesson 1

Contributing Teacher: Rob Gulson

Subject: Mathematics

Topic: Classifying Angles

Isolate –
identify the
core content

Key Concept	New Vocabulary
Identifying different types of angles	Acute, right, obtuse Straight, reflex, revolution

Room setup: Large open space such as a quadrangle or hall

Music suggestions: Bizarre Love Triangle by New Order, Love Triangle by Carnal Carnival, or Down on the Corner by Creedence Clearwater Revival

Equipment: Large signs with various angle types written on both sides. One side has the angle itself drawn underneath its name. The other only has the name of the angle.

Translate –
choose the
engagement
strategy

Phase One

Games—Competition

Separate students into teams of approximately six. Explain that each team will be challenged to make a series of different types of angles with their bodies, and here are the rules:

- When making the angles, students may lie on the ground, stand, or sit.
- Every student in the team must be involved in some way.
- The first team to correctly form the angle will win a point.
- The team with the most points at the end wins a prize.
- The teacher is the judge and has the final word.

Start by saying the name of the first angle, and holding up a sign with both the name and the drawing of the angle. After running through all of the angles a couple of times, switch to the sides with only the name. To keep it interesting, introduce variations, such as

Variation 1: When making the angle, students must not speak to each other.

Variation 2: Multiply—ask the teams to make two or three angles of the same type.

Variation 3: Diverge—give the teams two different angles to make at the same time.

Reinforce to students the need to be able to instantly identify different types of angles and know their classification. Ask students to discuss in their groups how to differentiate between an acute or obtuse angle and the reflex angle created. Suggest that this distinction be incorporated into their human diagrams.

After students have discussed the difference, pair up the teams. One team will form an angle, and the other team must discuss in their group which angle has been created. Switch roles. Repeat until all angles have been demonstrated at least once.

The primary memory strategy here is in the physical movement of the activity itself. This process will embed a strong kinesthetic memory of the different types of angles.

To reinforce the memory, take photographs during the activity and examples of the "human" angles to display around the room—appropriately labeled. Later on, you can use these photographs (minus their labels) for a highly entertaining review session, in which students are asked to identify the angles being created. The photos will act as a memory stimulus, provoking strong recall of the lesson.

Phase Two

Criticate encourage critical thinking

On their return to the classroom, start the critical thinking process by asking students to identify an example of each angle within the room. For example, the window contains several right angles, a vase holding flowers might form an acute angle facing the ceiling, or the clock is an angle of revolution. This conversation demonstrates that angles are not merely imaginary mathematical constructs—they exist everywhere in the physical world.

Next, ask students to work in their groups to discuss where an intimate understanding of the various types of angles might come in handy. For example, what role might an understanding of angles play for

- The shuttle reentering the atmosphere?

- Civil engineers surveying lots?

- Nautical navigation and positioning?

- The design and construction of a bridge?

- The trajectory of artillery shells shot from a cannon?

Or . . .

- Why is it important that the right angles of the window be precise—what might happen if they weren't cut exactly properly?

- Where might corresponding angles exist when railroad tracks cross a road?

Lesson 2

Contributing Teacher: Rob Gulson

Subject: Mathematics

Topic: Summary Statistics

Key Concept	New Vocabulary
Understanding the statistical process	Frequency histogram, cumulative frequency, box-and-whisker plot, frequency table, statistical process

Note: Students have already completed a general discussion covering various aspects of statistics, with a focus on analyzing data. This is a summary lesson used to reflect on these tools and explain the process by which statistical analysis occurs. Its purpose is for students to understand the logical flow of the statistical process.

Room setup: Desks arranged in groups of four, with all the below equipment

Music suggestions: *Count on Me* by The Doo Wops, *ABC* by The Jackson 5, *One Thing Leads to Another* by The Fixx, or *Rikki Don't Lose That Number* by Steely Dan

Equipment:
- 4 letter signs with the letters O, D, A, and P (per group)
- 1 worksheet with raw data and an accompanying question
- Frequency table
- Graph/grid paper
- Set of statistical measures

Phase One

Games—Competition

Students enter carrying only a pen, ruler, and calculator and sit together in groups of four. Ideally these groups have a mixture of abilities, allowing peer assistance. Ask students to review the equipment on their desk. Explain that, as a group, their goal is to find the answer to the question on their worksheet—however, they must follow a particular process.

Without any further explanation, ask each student to pick up one of the four letter signs. Then tell your students: "Congratulations! You have just chosen your role in the statistical process." In turn, ask the students holding each letter to stand up and hear what their role will be. Explain to each standing group what their letters stand for:

<u>A</u>nalyzer: completes a set of summary statistics on the task, including mean, median, mode, range, interquartile range, and standard deviation

<u>P</u>resenter: summarizes the data for the class and answers the question

<u>O</u>rganizer: takes the raw data and records it in the frequency table

<u>D</u>isplayer: takes this data from the table and puts it into the given format

Explain that as a team, students must now use the raw data on their table to answer the question on the worksheet. *But,* only one person may act at a time—the others can make suggestions, but the student with the letter must carry out his task. Students should think about and discuss what order to complete things in, bearing in mind that certain tasks cannot be undertaken *until others have been completed*.

Explain that the first step is to find the right order. In fact, the first group to put the letters in the correct order and hold them up to show the teacher will win a prize.

The order should be

Problem/Issue $\rightarrow$ Organize $\rightarrow$ Display $\rightarrow$ Analyze $\rightarrow$ **Present**
Solution

Jump on a chair and commentate to prompt the groups to get the order correct: for example, "In a bold move, the group by the door has A first—but how can they analyze data unless it's been organized?"

When all the groups have their cards in the correct order, challenge them to find the answer on their worksheet. Remind them that they must follow the order ODAP, and each step must be completed before the next one can begin.

Discuss why this order will work and give teams 2 minutes to come up with real-world situations where one or more of the stages of the process occur. You might start by asking, "Have you ever seen people in fluoro vests with clipboards counting cars at intersections? Where in the process of data analysis might they be at this point? What would come next?" Teams present their ideas back to the class.

Challenge each team to come up with an acrostic in 1 minute to help them remember the order of tasks in the statistical process. Give them one idea: Only Dress Appropriately Please. Each team must chant their acrostic to the class.

Phase Two

The task itself forces students to think critically about each aspect of the process as a separate and distinct stage. As they understand the *logical sequence* necessary for the proper analysis of any set of data, they will better understand the relationship between the steps. To reinforce the critical aspect of this lesson—understanding how each step is dependent on the previous one—two conversations can be introduced.

First, ask students to imagine someone trying to start a step in the process without the previous step being completed. For example, what might happen if one person tried to display the data before it was properly organized? Or what might happen if someone tried to analyze a set of data that had not been properly organized and displayed? In either situation, what problems might occur?

Second, to take this idea further, discuss with students other real-life situations such as the following where the *sequence* is critical to *success:*

- Not following a recipe in the proper order

- Assembling a bike

- Playing a football game without fully knowing the playbook

- Driving a car without having taken the time to get a license

- Take the test before studying

- Making an iPod playlist without having all of the songs

- Sending in a college application without first gathering the necessary documents, collecting letters of recommendation, and completing the forms

Lesson 3

Contributing Teacher: Rob Gulson

Subject: Mathematics

Topic: Coordinate Geometry

Key Concept	New Vocabulary
Applying coordinate geometry skills to higher level thinking problems	Cartesian plane, gradient formula, midpoint formula, distance formula

Note: Students have already completed several lessons on coordinate geometry, each focusing on one particular concept, such as locating and identifying the (x, y) coordinates of a point. The primary focus of this lesson is to demonstrate how these individual concepts can be combined to solve a more complex problem in geometry.

Room setup:	Tables pushed together for small-group work
Music suggestions:	*Turn, Turn, Turn* by The Byrds, *Go the Distance* by Faith Hill, or *The Formula* by The D.O.C.
Equipment:	• 1 question per group
	• 1 Cartesian plane per group
	• 1 pen per group
	• 1 calculator per group

Phase One

Introduce students to the new vocabulary: *Cartesian plane, gradient formula, midpoint formula,* and the *distance formula.*

Put students into small groups and ask them to explain each concept to each other. When all students agree they have a general understanding of the new terms, distribute the supplies and move the lesson to the next step.

Games—Competition

Give each group a different coordinate geometry problem to solve. These problems involve multiple steps. To complete the problem, students will need to use the skills they have learned previously. The rules for the activity are as follows:

- Only one person can write at a time.

- That person has 1 minute to make progress through the problem—a buzzer or bell will sound at the end of the minute—at which point the pen gets handed to the next person.

- This process repeats until the problem is solved.

- The first group to finish gets a prize.

Stress the importance of both working together and working systematically. Students should consider the following questions:

- "Where do I start?"

- "What is it asking me to do?"

- "Why did it ask me to do this part of the problem at this point— what have I learned that I can use to solve the next step?"

During the process, students will be talking to each other and must identify the process needed to solve each stage of the problem. As you walk around the room, encourage students to discuss the approach they would take to solving that part of the problem, *even if they are not the person holding the pen.*

This lesson has a memory strategy built into the flow of the activity— the conversation and discussion revolve around how to solve that step of the problem. As students work together to offer and discard various strategies, and eventually work together to select the proper one, they are constantly revisiting the strategy they will use later *individually* as they solve complex problems. They are recognizing the importance of considering various options, selecting the correct one, and ultimately developing a structured and systematic approach to problem solving.

Phase Two

Every aspect of the activity requires students to work together to think critically. They are constantly assessing, appraising, and evaluating various lines of reasoning to solve the problem, and while doing so are detecting inconsistencies, mistakes, and errors in each other's arguments. After one or two rotations it becomes clear that students cannot simply pick up the pen and do their minute without understanding what was done previously. This encourages them to actively think ahead in the process about challenges or questions that might arise when it becomes their turn.

At the end of the activity, to cement their critical thinking, ask each group to come up with at least one helpful hint they would offer to others about how to answer complex problems, and one typical error students should be aware of when solving this type of problem. All students can copy these down to assist them in the future. Finally, the lesson ends with all students individually completing the same complex coordinate geometry problem and then pairing up to share the process they used to generate their answer.

In future class sessions, this idea might be reinforced by the teacher showing a complex coordinate geometry problem and asking, "Discuss with others near you the process you would use to solve this problem." The key is that they don't have to actually solve it mathematically—the purpose is merely to make sure they frequently revisit the idea of *how* to solve these types of problems.

Lesson 4

Contributing Teacher: Rob Gulson

Subject: Mathematics

Topic: Irregular Areas, Offset Surveys, Field Diagrams

Key Concept	New Vocabulary
Using field diagrams to calculate areas of irregularly sized blocks	Offset survey, field diagram

Room setup: Large outdoor area, such as a hall, oval, or quadrangle. In the classroom, tables for small-group work. *The teacher wears a hard hat and a fluoro bib (a fluorescent vest of the type used for doing construction work, also used in some sporting activities).*

Music suggestions: *Back on the Chain Gang* by The Pretenders, *Fields of Gold* by Sting, or *Love Is a Battlefield* by Pat Benatar

Equipment:
- 1 fluoro bib and hard hat for teacher
- 1 fluoro bib per group
- 1 trundle wheel per group
- 1 tape measure plane per group
- At least 4 ground markers/cones per group

Phase One

Props

Without explaining your attire, quickly introduce the concept of an offset survey—*a small area measured perpendicularly from a main survey line.* Explain that offset surveys are used most frequently to measure irregular shapes. The students will be using a hands-on approach to create an actual offset survey. It will allow them to understand conceptually what these types of surveys are, as well as to see how they work in the physical environment.

- Group students into teams of about five.
- Give one student in each group a fluoro bib and tell that student that he or she is the "foreman."

- Give the foreman a map with an irregular area drawn to a 1 inch = 1 yard scale.

- Ask the foreman to send volunteers to pick up measuring instruments and ground markers for each group.

Before moving the class outside, set out the ground rules:

- Each team must first calculate the measurements of their irregular area.

- Then teams use the measuring devices and ground markers to create an accurate life-sized version of the irregular area on the school oval/hall/quadrangle.

- The foreman oversees the project and is responsible for his or her group completing the task in a timely manner.

When each group has created its irregular area, the groups must now create an actual offset survey of each irregular area created by the other groups. Groups rotate between irregular areas until they have created an offset survey of any area they did not construct. When all groups are finished, students return to the classroom.

Back in the classroom, explain to your students that an offset survey is usually a roughly drawn representation of an actual irregular sized area. They must now take the offset surveys they created of the other groups' areas and—using graph paper for accuracy—create a *field diagram*—a scaled diagram of each area. Students work in groups to create field diagrams of each of the other irregular areas. When these are completed, they can compare them with the ones other groups have created, and then to the original field diagram given to each group at the start of the lesson.

Students will have been talking throughout the above activity. However, now specifically ask teams to discuss the idea that they have been introduced to the three-part cycle of offset surveys. Challenge each team to come up with a diagram showing the relationship between the three elements. They should end up with something like this:

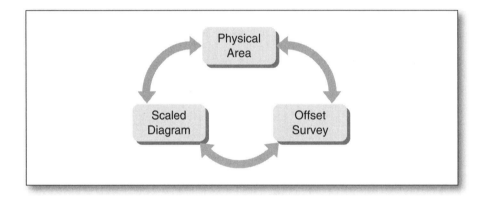

Discuss the idea that any one part should be enough to understand the other two parts, meaning, for example, that from measuring the actual physical area, a person should be able to do an offset survey, and from this create a scaled field diagram. Or, from a scaled field diagram, a person should have an excellent idea of what the actual area looks like.

The activity itself has many built-in memory devices. Students talking to each other about the maps they are creating allows auditory learners to articulate and clarify their ideas. In the same way, comparing and contrasting their creations allows these learners to make error corrections and refine their thinking. Making actual offset surveys and field diagrams—not just one but several of them—allows visual learners to cement their understandings. For kinesthetic learners, the physical engagement component of the activity—going outside, constructing the irregular areas, measuring the areas—is not only critical to keeping them engaged in the activity; it will help with recall later.

All of these strategies are important since, in math especially, some students occasionally find it difficult to take the theoretical and make it practical. In this lesson, however, allowing these groups of students to manually construct the irregular areas from the measurements they have been given is a much more concrete way for them to understand the idea of what an *offset survey* represents, which will lead to better recall. And creating an actual offset survey from the irregular areas made by other groups of students—and from that developing a *field diagram*—clearly demonstrates the relationship between these concepts, again not only increasing students' understanding in the short term, but helping long-term recall.

Phase Two

Criticate
encourage
critical
thinking

Challenge students to come up with examples in which offset surveys might be found in the real world. Would they be needed in the construction industry? If so, where and how? On a smaller scale, would they be important in the development of residential areas? Again, where, why, and how? Would they play any role in creating national parks?

One of the key aspects of critical thinking is learning through reflection and error correction. Students were engaged in error correction when comparing their offset survey notes with each other and with the team that originally constructed each area to determine the accuracy of their field drawings. Now, you can expand on this idea. Work with students to consider the real world, and the implications of errors made when creating an offset survey, or errors made when creating a field drawing from an offset survey.

Ask students what problems might emerge if these seemingly small errors were made on a much larger scale. What might be the effect of a 1-cm error on the map of a large ranch, for example, where 1 inch = 10 miles? What might happen if a plot of land for constructing a new building is measured incorrectly? Additionally, and perhaps more important, discuss *how* errors might be made by individuals creating these field diagrams. What factors might affect the accuracy of their measurements, and how can these potential errors be avoided?

Another avenue of critical thinking to be explored, especially given that this is a math class, could be *measurement*. Ask students how they could calculate the area of these irregular-sized blocks of land. They should be able to see from their diagrams' areas that these composite shapes can be broken up into smaller, more regular shapes. Students should already know the formulas needed to calculate the area of each of these shapes and see that the sum of these areas would be the area of the irregular shape. This challenge allows them to bring multiple mathematical ideas to bear on a single problem—which is often the case in the real world.

Lesson 5

Contributing Teacher: Rob Gulson

Subject: Mathematics

Topic: Operations With Directed Numbers

Key Concept	New Vocabulary
Addition and subtraction of directed numbers	Directed numbers, positive and negative numbers, number lines

Room setup: Chairs and tables cleared to the side of the room; a number line (from –10 to +10) made from masking tape and drawn in chalk on the floor of the classroom

Music suggestions: *The Sign* by Ace of Base, *I Walk the Line* by Johnny Cash, *Opposites Attract* by Paula Abdul, or *You've Got My Number* by the Undertones

Equipment: Masking tape and chalk to create the number line

Phase One

Games (TV)

When students arrive for class, invite them to take a moment and walk around the *number line,* simply to check it out. When they are seated again, introduce the concept of *directed numbers—numbers that have both a size and a direction.* For example, –5, 8, 100, –100, –3.5, 0.33, and –0.75 are all directed numbers.

Introduce students to (or remind them of) the idea of *positive* and *negative* numbers. Demonstrate where these different types of number are located on the number line.

Select one student to "Come on Down" to the number line. Using the number line, the student must answer a series of math questions by standing on the correct answer. Students can do this by themselves, or other students can be encouraged to help. To sustain the TV game show analogy, tell the selected students they can phone a friend or use their brain trust.

Make sure the math problems range in difficulty, starting with simple ones and then gradually getting more challenging. The following three-step sequence is useful to help students gently build their understanding of this concept:

1. First, simply ask the student to locate and stand on a number on the number line. For example, ask the student to stand on

   3, then **−2,** then **7,** and then **−1.**

2. Next, ask the student to solve simple calculations—meaning ones that *do not* have a "+" and "−" next to each other. For example,

   −3 + 5 = ?   or   **2 − 7 = ?**   or   **−8 + 5 = ?**

3. Finally, invite the student to do more complicated calculations—meaning ones that *do* have a "+" and "−" next to each other. For example,

   1 + −5 = ?   or   **2 − 4 = ?**   or   **−2 + −5 = ?**

After seeing a few examples in the second and third steps of this sequence, everyone will typically start seeing a pattern to the movements used to solve the problem. At this point, pause the activity and introduce your students to *SDS*—a memory device they can use to answer these questions. The SDS approach stands for

Start: Where do I *start* on the number line?

Direction: Which *direction* am I moving on the line?

Spaces: How many *spaces* am I moving?

For example, in the question below, notice how the correct answer can be found by following the **SDS** approach:

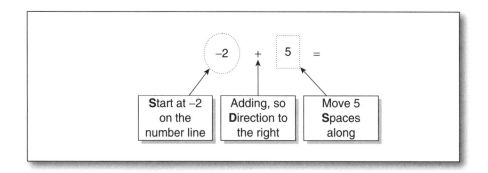

From this point on, as other students step to the number line for their turn, ask them to use the SDS sequence and say it *out loud* as they move. If possible, allow all students to do several examples on the number line, especially the more complicated ones. Each time, ask them to say the SDS sequence out loud.

When all students have had an opportunity to be on the number line, ask the class what they noticed about how students moved when doing problems from the *third* step of the sequence. After discussing this briefly with them, explain that the idea can be clarified and simplified by stating that

the "+" and "−" are—GASP—in a *relationship!*

Consider as an example 2 + −3. Dialogue to explain these two symbols being next to each other might go something like this:

"The '+' and '−' are right next door to each other, which means they are having a relationship. Unfortunately, *they just have nothing in common!* They are just too dissimilar, so their relationship is destined for failure. That will be really sad—it'll be really *negative.* Therefore, 2 + −3 = 2 − 3."

Or consider the example 5 − (−3). Dialogue to explain the change might go something like this:

The "−" and "−" are right next door to each other, which means they are having a relationship. Luckily they just really click—*they seem to have everything in common!* They are perfect together, so their relationship will flourish. That will be really happy for them—it'll be really *positive*. Therefore, $5 - (-3) = 5 + 3$.

Ask students to explain this idea to a group or partner. Then write several problems on the board where these signs appear next to each other and explain how to solve them using this idea. Finally, let students work with a partner on several more problems that have these signs next to each other. While figuring out the problems, they must be using the SDS approach as well as explaining to each other what to do with the signs using language similar to that in the examples shown above. Note that although most groups of students will be working together at their desks, *one group should always be doing the activity using the actual number line* to further reinforce their understanding of the idea.

Once the basic idea is clear to most students, it may be useful to challenge them in a new and creative way to cement their understanding of this idea and their confidence that they can solve these problems. To do this, *give students the answers* to a few problems and allow them to work *backward* to discover the steps they would typically need to do to solve them. To do this, students will need to identify patterns that exist in each problem, and the usefulness of the SDS concept will become even more clear.

To reinforce the basic strategy—and expand it out to *larger* number lines—create a game using a larger number line. Ask each student to draw a larger number line on a sheet of paper, perhaps one that goes from –100 to +100. Then ask a series of questions (similar to ones from the second and third steps of the learning sequence), and ask students to work out the answer using the number line they created. Introduce competition by challenging students to be the first to get the correct answer. This engaging activity encourages students to keep cool under pressure while solving math problems. You could even have a series of knockout rounds and end the game by crowning one student "The Number Line King"!

Memory strategies are woven throughout the above activities section. Using the large number line on the floor is certainly an excellent visual learning device. However, it is equally important for kinesthetic learners in the group, as they have a chance to physically move in the classroom while working out a problem. Learning through discussion with a partner is helpful to almost all students when later attempting to recall the key ideas.

The SDS acronym—*start*, *direction*, and *space*—is a simple yet powerful memory device. It becomes quickly embedded in memory as students refer back to this idea repeatedly when initially learning this concept, since it helps them clarify the basic idea, gives them a clear starting point, and provides a specific linear sequence for solving the equation.

Phase Two

Now it's time to expand student thinking beyond the boundaries of the classroom and consider where this concept might show up in the real world. To do so, first ask students where they have seen negative numbers, and why this idea might be important. After a brief discussion, offer some specific team challenges where negative and positive numbers come into play. For example:

- Suppose your school does not open on any day when the temperature is below –22°C at 7:00 a.m. You wake up at 4:00 a.m. and the temperature is –34°C. It looks like you can stay warm in bed! How many degrees must the temperature rise before your day gets ruined in the next 3 hours and school opens?

- Imagine your checking account had $236 in it when you last looked at it on Monday. Since then you've written three checks for $47, $102, and $76. It's Friday, and you think you'll need $40 in spending money for the weekend, so you're about to write a check for that amount. But you have to be careful— if you don't have enough money in your account, the bank will charge you a $25 fee, and you can't afford that. Can you write the check or not?

- A teacher tells you he has been teaching for almost 20 years. However, you know he was also a salesman for 7 years and worked in construction for another 12 years. Yet you know for a fact that this teacher is 51 years old. Given this information, how old must he have been when he started teaching? And more important, *what might this tell you about him as a teacher?*

These types of examples will help students expand their thinking about positive and negative numbers and the importance of understanding number lines as they apply to the real world.

Lesson 6

Contributing Teacher: Rob Gulson

Subject: Mathematics

Topic: Consumer Arithmetic: Wages and Salaries

Key Concept	New Vocabulary
Comparing wages, salaries, and working conditions	Wage, salary, overtime, vacation pay

Room setup: Students arrive to find their classroom set up like a waiting area. At the front of the class is a large sign saying "Employment Agency." The teacher is wearing a suit.

Music suggestions: *Money* by Pink Floyd, *Money, Money, Money* by ABBA, *Money Burns a Hole in My Pocket* by Dean Martin, or *Take the Money and Run* by The Steve Miller Band

Equipment: A collection of job advertisements

Phase One

Props

Organize students into groups of three or four, and give each group a different job advertisement. Each group has 10 minutes to develop a short presentation that sells this particular job to the rest of the class. Explain that students are playing the role of employers. The rest of the class are potential employees, looking for the best job available.

Give specific guidelines for what the presentations should cover:

- State whether the employee will be paid a *wage* or a *salary*

- The rate of pay per annum, per month, per week, and per hour

- Overtime pay

- Vacation pay

- Lifestyle benefits, if any

Clarify what each of these terms means, making sure you explain the concept of *lifestyle benefits*—nonmonetary benefits such as flexible working hours or free child care. This final concept allows students to be more creative and imaginative when it comes to creating their presentation and selling their job. Here they can be prompted to consider working hours, outdoors versus indoors, or working conditions.

While students are working, wander about the class and prompt groups to be as creative as possible when preparing their presentation. If needed, call the class together to discuss how to calculate the relative pay per period.

When all groups have given their presentations, each student writes down which job he or she would choose and why. Each student must give at least two reasons why that job was the most appealing compared with the others—and at least one of those answers must be *mathematical*. This will encourage students to consider how to compare different pay periods (annual, monthly, weekly, and hourly), and how wage and salary payments differ.

Give students a few moments to compare their decisions with the decisions of those seated about them—and make adjustments if necessary. Students take turns standing and explaining their choices and the reasons behind them. Finally, you can lead a general conversation about how the various decisions were made, how pay salaries were compared, and what factors seemed to influence people the most.

This lesson has no content requiring rote memorization. However, it has numerous built-in memory strategies thanks to the high level of talking, thinking, and engagement required to carry out the above activity.

In addition, because it uses actual job advertisements, the activity has a heightened sense of credibility. Its natural connection to real-life scenarios significantly increases its impact, making it far more tangible to students—and thus more memorable.

Phase Two

This lesson is unusual in that, rather than leaving the heavy-duty critical thinking until the end, the entire activity is built on the critical-thinking principles. To start with, there *is no right answer to this activity*. Instead, it guides students to

- Assess, appraise, and evaluate various lines of reasoning.

- Detect inconsistencies and potential errors in logic when listening to the presentations and when listening to how other students made their decisions.

- Identify the relative importance of ideas when they consider what factors are most important to others—and what factors are most important to them—when making and defending a job choice.

- Identify and evaluate the relative importance of their ideas when justifying their own decision.

Considering a job for more than just the money to be earned from it can be an abstract idea for high school students. Encouraging them to think beyond the dollar forces them to critically evaluate both the position they are trying to sell during their presentation and their position when making a decision.

ENGLISH

Lesson 1

Contributing Teacher: John Tzantzaris

Subject: English

Lesson: Love in Shakespeare's *Othello*

Isolate —
identify the
core content

Key Concept	New Vocabulary
What variations of love are demonstrated in the play *Othello*?	Patriarchy Paternal Homosocial Platonic Unrequited

Room setup: If possible, tables and chairs pushed to the edges of the room, so students have room to move into pairs and work standing up

Music suggestions: *Jealous Guy* by John Lennon/Roxy Music, *Jessie's Girl* by Rick Springfield, or *Hey Jealousy* by The Gin Blossoms

Equipment:
- Box containing enough cards for each student, with a mix of the main characters from *Othello:* Desdemona, Othello, Brabantio, Roderigo, Cassio, Emilia, and Iago

- Box containing enough cards for each student, with a mix of the 5 new vocabulary theme concepts: *paternal* love, *affection* between friends, *unrequited* love, *homosocial* love, and *elevated* sexual love

Translate —
choose the
engagement
strategy

Phase One

Props

Students take one card each from both boxes. Give them a moment to share the cards they pulled out with the students near them.

Explain that love is a central concern in the play and motivates many of the characters' actions. Spend some time here discussing the five primary variations on love written down on the cards the

students have selected. Where possible, make references to how the different types of love emerge in the play.

Now, ask students to closely think about the character and the variation of love they have selected. Ask them to consider privately for a moment what is revealed about love and the relationships their character has with others.

Now, ask students to discuss their findings with a partner. They should refer to specific moments in the play as much as possible. In this discussion, students should introduce their character and their specific variation of love to the other students and outline how this is demonstrated in the play.

Finally, students report back to the group on their partner's character and variation of love. Other students are invited to comment on the accuracy of the report.

Ask students to create their own map of the key relationships in *Othello* by writing down the five new vocabulary words in their notes and then joining the relevant character names to the words. Ask students to use different colors for each word and in some way visually demonstrate the relationship between the character pairs. For example, draw a love heart with a cross through it for unrequited love; or draw large and small stick figures for paternal love. Draw your own map on the board, but let students come up with their own creative representations.

Phase Two

Think More About the Themes

Organize students into five groups—perhaps group them according to the theme cards they received in the first activity. For example, "Everyone with a paternal love card, get into a group by the door."

Give each group an excerpt from the play that relates to one of the five variations on the theme of love.

Ask students to identify what type of love is being explored in the excerpt. They need to identify key words and phrases that reflect that particular type of love, and write them on the board.

Ask each group to find two to three more examples of their variation of love in the play and present them to the whole class.

Make the Themes Current

Ask each group to come up with at least two other examples of their type of love, but this time in current pop culture, such as TV shows, movies, or songs.

Using these examples, groups discuss the potential benefits—and costs—of each type of love in the various situations.

Buried Gems: Many lessons never move beyond the borders of the specific area of study. In this case, ending the lesson by expanding into the world of pop culture—a world much more familiar to high school students—adds depth to the lesson.

Lesson 2

Contributing Teacher: John Tzantzaris

Subject: English

Lesson: Writing Description

Key Concept	New Vocabulary
Writing descriptions of a person	Omniscient narration Visual imagery Aural imagery Senses

Room setup: A desk for each student in any configuration

Music suggestions: *Sensory Overload* by Bad Religion, *I Can See Clearly Now* by Johnny Nash, *Smells Like Teen Spirit* by Nirvana, *Words* by Train, or *Words* by The Bee Gees

Equipment:
- Basket or box
- Slips of paper to write each student's name on

Phase One

First, introduce students to the key vocabulary terms, explaining each one in terms of the effect it has on the brain. For example, the phrase *visual imagery* refers to the flow of thoughts we can see, hear, feel, smell, or taste—a way the mind encodes, stores, and expresses information.

Next, write up a list of physical features on the board. For example:

- Eyes
- Ears
- Hair
- Height
- Weight
- Nose
- Skin

Ask students to brainstorm at least five descriptive words for each physical feature with a partner. Walk around the room challenging students to find stronger—more creative—descriptors. For example, for hair, instead of *balding*, the suggestion might be *receding*.

Props

Each student writes his or her name on a slip of paper. These slips are folded and placed in a basket. At random each student selects *one* piece of paper from the basket. Ask students not to reveal the name of the student listed on their slip of paper.

Remind students that successful creative writing involves studying one's subject very closely. They must be able to *paint* a clear picture for their reader using words. Students now walk about the room and—without revealing who their subject is—note as many of their distinctive features as possible.

Students must now write a paragraph, based on an imaginary event, that the chosen subject is involved in. They must describe the person in the third person, using *omniscient narration*, and cannot use the student's name.

Before they start, to avoid the clichéd school scenarios, it may prove helpful to brainstorm some imaginary events for students to use in their paragraphs. In addition, introduce students to the idea of attempting to *show* the reader instead of *telling* the reader.

Finally, students read their paragraphs aloud one at a time. Each time, ask the class to guess the person being described by writing his or her name on a piece of paper. The correct subject of each description is revealed at the end of the lesson.

The memory strategy used in this lesson is a simple one—repetition. As students listen to each other's paragraphs in an attempt to decide which student is being described, over and over they are focusing on the descriptive words and phrases being used, and thus reinforcing their understanding of the lesson. In the process, they are developing their imaginative skills for writing descriptive passages.

Phase Two

Ask students to rewrite a given passage using more descriptive words that *show* instead of *tell*. When the exercise is complete, students share with each other what they have written. At this point it will become clear that showing instead of telling by using more descriptive language allows readers to work things out for themselves, creating a more powerful, personalized image.

Now students return to the paragraph they had previously written describing one of the class members in an imaginary scene and reflect on how well their paragraph shows instead of tells. In pairs, they edit their original paragraphs focusing on the *show not tell* approach. When students have completed their original descriptive passage, they tape it as well as the edited version to the wall, and all students walk around reading and comparing the different versions.

Finally, the entire class discusses where descriptive writing shows up in the everyday world. For example, advertisements frequently use descriptive writing to grab our attention. Or why are some novels more popular than others? Usually, the more popular ones appeal to a larger audience because of the creative, imaginative, descriptive language used.

Lesson 3

Contributing Teacher: Derrice Randall

Subject: English

Lesson: Plot Development

Key Concept	New Vocabulary
Identify key stages of plot development Identify the supporting text passages of events or scenes within each stage	Plot development Exposition, rising action, climax, falling action, and conclusion Text passages

Note: Before this lesson, students have already learned the memory pegging system (see Chapter 5) and read the book to be analyzed in the lesson.

Room setup: Groups of tables where four students can work together

Music suggestions: *Bedtime Story* by Madonna, *Ghost Story* by Sting, *The Inside Story* by Terri Clark, or *Never Ending Story* by Limahl

Equipment: Four sets of cards, each set containing 5 or 6 picture cards all related to a common theme. For example, one set of cards might focus on a family—one picture shows them packing the car, another shows them at the beach, another shows them eating, and so on. Another set of cards might focus on a bear—one picture shows him fishing in a stream, another shows him scratching his back, and another shows him hibernating.

Phase One

Stories

Organize students in groups of four or five, and give each team a set of cards.

Challenge teams to arrange their set of cards into a sequence that visually tells a story—wait until all teams have a workable sequence.

Next, ask each team to develop a verbal explanation—*words*—of their story. This entire process should take no more than 3 minutes—a brief verbal overview will suffice.

Teams share their stories with other groups, explaining why the cards are in the order shown, and telling them what words they came up with to help further explain their story. Groups then exchange their set of cards with another group, and the process is repeated two or three more times.

Explain that they have just participated in *plot development*. However, there are actually five distinct stages in the development of any plot: exposition, rising action (or complication), climax, falling action (or denouement), and conclusion. Write these terms on the board so students can see them clearly, and discuss each one briefly.

Still in their teams, ask students to work together to identify the five basic stages of a novel they are all familiar with. Periodically, pause the discussion to check in and make sure the teams are on track. If needed, you might ask teams to share their ideas so far, or ask leading questions until all groups have a basic sense of the five general plot development stages in this particular story.

Now explain there are usually several key elements within each stage. These elements are events or scenes that are fundamental to the flow of that stage. Remind students that, when creating their own stories in the opening activity, they added words to help explain the story. This is exactly what authors do—they add words in the form of *text passages* to explain the story. Ask students to go back and jot down at least three important events or scenes within each stage. Allow 5 minutes only.

Take 2 minutes and ask students to stand up and work in pairs or trios to remind each other of the 20 memory pegs they learned earlier in the year.

Next, explain they can use these memory pegs to help remember the stages of plot development—as well as key elements of each stage— of any story. As an example, ask them to consider the children's classic story *The Three Little Pigs*. Now show them the following way the pegs could be used to remember this story:

1. A story can only start ONE time—**Exposition**

2. The pigs only had TWO options—Stay home or leave the nest

3. The THREE little pigs were close siblings

4. There were FOUR characters in the story

5. The sun rises at FIVE in the morning—**Rising Action**

6. At SIX o'clock the pigs set off on an adventure

7. It was UP to the pigs to decide what kind of house they wanted to build

8. The pigs worked madly to build their houses, their arms whirling like an OCTOPUS

9. At the top of the LINE is the **Climax**

10. Then came the COWARDLY (chicken) wolf

11. No FENCE could protect the pigs

12. The **1**st **2** pigs' houses BROKE into pieces

13. The wolf was UNLUCKY in getting in the pigs—**Falling Action**

14. The third pig's LOVE for his brothers caused him to let them in

15. The wolf's FAMED huffing didn't work

16. The wolf's unsuccessful efforts DROVE him crazy

17. The story READ differently with the 3rd pig's house— **Conclusion**

18. The wolf CHECKED out the chimney as his final option

19. The wolf only had a REMOTE chance of this plan working

20. The other 2 pigs could CLEARLY SEE that the 3rd pig built the best house and had had the better plan

Note: Don't ask students to memorize this list—it's simply a demonstration of how to break up and peg a story.

Now invite students to apply the same idea to the story they've been working on. Ask them to peg the stages and elements of each stage using this memory strategy. Put the above list on the board, so students can refer to it while creating their own.

After all groups have completed their 20 items, ask each group to stand and share what they created. This often leads to great laughter— leading to great learning!

Phase Two

In Language Arts, the overarching goal is often for students to be able to question, challenge, and explain everything they read or write.

To further develop their awareness in this specific area of plot development, ask students a series of *why* questions revolving around the importance of plot development. For example:

Did the exposition stage grab your attention? If so, why? If not, why not?

Did any of the stages drag on too long, or were they too short?

Why do you believe the author chose particular events or scenes to tell a particular stage of the story?

In your opinion, were any of the events or scenes unnecessary to the plot development?

Think of at least two other events or scenes that could be added to that stage that might have explained it *even better*.

Was the conclusion stage rewarding and fulfilling, and did it bring the story to a satisfying end? If not, what could have been done differently?

Were any questions left unanswered? If so, do you think this was something the author did deliberately? Why?

SCIENCE

Lesson 1

Contributing Teacher: J. P. Friend

Subject: Biology

Lesson: Surface-Area-to-Volume Ratio

Key Concept	New Vocabulary
How surface-area-to-volume ratio relates to cell size	Surface-area-to-volume ratio Diffusion Membrane

Note: This lesson is the second in a series on this topic. Students already have some background knowledge and have performed an experiment explaining the basics of the concept of *surface-area-to-volume ratio.*

Room setup: Tennis court or asphalt area drawn with circles and arranged with boxes as shown below:

4-m circle   6-m circle   8-m circle
□ = Boxes

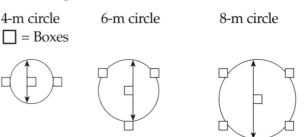

Music suggestions: *Cell Block Tango* on the Chicago soundtrack, *Scratching the Surface* by The Hourglass, or *Tainted Love* by Soft Cell (explain who the artist is afterward to get the groan factor)

Equipment:
- Chalk
- 4-m + 6-m + 8-m-diameter chalk circles on the asphalt
- Timer
- 12 buckets or boxes (9 full of screwed-up paper)
- Groups of 4, 6, and 8 students

Phase One

Games—Competition

Take students outside and show them the setup of boxes and circles. Assign students to each area: four to the 4-m circle, six to the

6-m circle, and eight to the 8-m circle. With no explanation, tell students they will have 1 minute to move as many pieces of paper as possible from the *outside boxes* to the *inside box*. The pieces of paper must be moved one at a time and must be placed inside the box—not thrown.

After 1 minute, stop the activity and ask students to count the number of pieces of paper in the box in the middle of each circle. Repeat this a couple of times for reliability. The process becomes quite competitive, but the results are always the same: the small circle wins. You can also do the activity in reverse, with a large box in the middle and the paper being moved out. The results will still be the same.

Bring your students back to the classroom and ask them if they can think of any biological process the activity might mimic. They usually articulate quite quickly that the activity is strikingly similar to the idea of *surface-area-to-volume ratio* concept previously introduced regarding cell size.

Ask students to work in pairs or trios to identify what each part of the activity represented. Walk around to support their thinking. Try to help them realize the following:

The chalk circle represents a cell membrane.

The paper is material moving into and out of the cell.

The process of moving through the membrane is called *diffusion*.

Debrief this activity with a concrete illustration, including a visual, such as this:

> *"The ratio between the surface area and volume of cells and organisms has a tremendous impact on their biology. Many aquatic microorganisms have <u>increased surface area</u> to increase their drag in the water. Why? Because this reduces their 'rate of sink' and allows them to remain near the surface with less energy expenditure."*

Because this lesson incorporates movement, competition, laugher, and teamwork—and partly because it takes place *outside*—the activity performed by the students is highly memorable on its own. When asked later to recount what the activity was, and what it represented, many are able to do so easily. However, to complete the learning, the key point of the lesson must also be remembered. At this point, for complete clarity, the teacher writes on the board the following statement:

> *"A small cell <u>equals</u> a high surface-area-to-volume ratio <u>equals</u> efficient diffusion."*

Give groups of students 3 minutes to invent a memory strategy. Then each group shares their memory strategy with the other groups.

For example, one group might make the sentence into a creative rhyme while another group might make the sentence into a lyric and sing it. Another group might make the sentence into a silly short story such as this one:

"A small cell on the *equator* sat on a high surface and boldly told the volume ratio, 'I'm *equal* to the task of *efficient diffusion!*'"

Phase Two

Challenge groups or pairs to answer questions about the positive or negative effects of having high surface area or low surface area. For example:

- Name at least three reasons why an increased surface area to volume ratio might be dangerous. (*Answers: (1) it means increased exposure to the environment, (2) it increases loss of water and dissolved substances, and (3) it presents problems of temperature control in unfavorable environments.*)

- Jellyfish have many tentacles, which means increased surface area. Why is this necessary for their survival? (*Answer: Greater surface area allows more of the surrounding water to be sifted for nutrients.*)

- Why do you think our lungs have numerous branches? (*Answer: It increases the surface area through which oxygen is passed into the blood and carbon dioxide is released from the blood.*)

- Can you think of any other human organs that have increased surface area? Why? (*One answer: The intestine has a finely wrinkled internal surface, increasing the area through which nutrients are absorbed by the body.*)

- Based on what we have learned about surface-to-volume ratios and assuming that humans lose heat from their skin, how would you explain why parents wrap up an infant and cover its head on days when they will go out in shirtsleeves? (*Answer: Since babies are smaller than adults and have the same basic shape, they have a **larger** surface area to volume ratio than adults. If humans lose heat through their skin and babies have more skin per unit volume, they will lose heat more quickly than an adult.*)

- Animals such as flatworms and leeches can rely on diffusion for absorption and rejection of respiratory gases, but humans can't do the same thing. Why? (*Answer: Those animals have more surface area per unit volume.*)

Lesson 2

Contributing Teacher: J. P. Friend

Subject: Science

Lesson: Order of Levers

Key Concept	New Vocabulary
To understand and identify 1st-, 2nd-, and 3rd-order levers	1st-, 2nd-, and 3rd-order levers Load, effort, and fulcrum

Note: Students have previously been introduced to the idea of load, effort, and fulcrum, so these terms are not entirely new to them.

Room setup: Before the lesson, place a number of levers around the room at numbered stations.

Music suggestions: *I Like to Move It* by Crazy Frog, *I Feel the Earth Move* by Carole King, or *Love Machine* by The Miracles

Equipment: 10 examples or diagrams of levers—for example, scissors, wire cutters, nutcrackers, bolt cutters, a door handle, ice tongs, a crowbar, a jawbone, a bicycle brake handle, and a crescent wrench

Phase One

Part 1

Give students some direct instruction about the three orders of levers, and offer them the following simple way to remember the difference between them.

"F, L, E, easy as 1, 2, 3!"

Ask students to repeat the phrase ("F, L, E" is pronounced "Flee!"). They must say it several times and be sure they know it before the lesson continues.

Now explain the saying:

If the fulcrum (F) is in the middle, it is a 1st-order lever.

If the load (L) is in the middle, it is a 2nd-order lever.

If the effort (E) is in the middle, it is a 3rd-order lever.

Show your students visuals of several examples to clarify this idea. For example:

- Seesaw/wire cutters—1st-order lever (fulcrum in the middle)

- Wheelbarrow/nutcracker—2nd-order lever (load in the middle)

- Construction crane/tweezers—3rd-order lever (effort in the middle)

Ask students to identify what order of lever they are seeing, what makes them think it's that order, and where the other two parts of the lever are. For example, in a 3rd-order lever, where are the load and fulcrum? When most students have grasped the difference between the three orders of levers, the lesson moves into the next step.

Props

Ask students to construct the following table:

Station	Name of Object	Diagram of Object	Order of Lever
1			
2			

Divide students into an even number of pairs or trios and give them a station to start at. Give them approximately 2 minutes at each station to complete the table. Remind students to use the mnemonic device introduced at the start of the lesson to help them classify the type of lever at each station. Use a signal—perhaps a bell, buzzer, or song—to indicate it's time to move to the next station.

When all groups have visited all stations, ask them to join up with the next group and review their findings with each other. Are they the same or different? If any answers do not match, they must all return to that station and come to a common agreement as to the answer.

Assign each group with a station to report back on. After 2 minutes of preparation time, each pair talks about that station, stating the order of lever and justifying why they say it belongs to that order. At the end of each report, the rest of the class indicates whether they agree or disagree with the decision and why.

Part 2

The mnemonic device introduced at the start of the lesson is a simple and powerful way to remember the differences between the three types of levers. While students are visiting the stations, they are usually muttering "F, L, E, easy as 1, 2, 3," thereby reinforcing their memory of this device. After the activity is complete, through multiple repetitions of this saying—enhanced by discussion and experimentation—students are usually easily able to remember the difference between the three orders of levers.

In a way, mnemonic devices are actually levers—simple machines that help students remember more information, more easily, than they could on their own. Noting this to them near the end of the lesson is a humorous way to remind them of the mnemonic device and its usefulness in keeping the three types of levers distinct from each other.

Phase Two

Challenge students with a series of questions related to orders of levers—not simple identification questions, but ones that will require some refection and decision making on their part. Each time, pose the question first, and then ask students to talk to a partner before making a decision. Make sure they are ready to defend their decision with sound reasoning.

Questions might be along the lines of the following:

- The famous Greek philosopher Archimedes is reported to have said, "Give me a lever long enough, and I will move the world!" What did he mean by this statement? (*Answer: If a lever is long enough—and strong enough—it can lift almost any weight.*)

- Two children want to go on a seesaw. One child weights 50 lbs., and the other weights 80 lbs. To balance the seesaw, which child should move closer to the middle? (*Answer: The heavier child.*)

- Do you agree or disagree with the following statement: The human arm is a 3rd-order lever. (*Answer: Yes, because the bending of the elbow is caused by the contraction of the bicep muscle.*)

Lesson 3

Teacher: J. P. Friend

Subject: Science

Lesson: Transverse and Longitudinal (Compression) Waves

Isolate –
identify the
core content

Key Concept	New Vocabulary
Transverse and longitudinal (compression) waves as they relate to sound and light	Transverse waves Longitudinal waves Compression waves

Room setup: A large enough space for all students to stand in a continuous line

Music suggestions: *Surfin' Safari* and *Catch a Wave* by The Beach Boys, *Wipeout* by The Safaris, or *Heat Wave* by Martha Reeves

Equipment: • Several long pieces of ribbon or string

• Several Slinky toys

Translate –
choose the
engagement
strategy

Phase One

Props

Announce that this lesson will begin with an activity. Explain that the activity will *not* make sense at first, but definitely will later. For now, students' only job is to participate and notice what people are doing.

First, ask students to stand in a continuous line across the room with an arm's length between each student. Then ask them to turn so they are each facing the back of the student in front of them. Next, ask the student at the head of the line to take one gentle *light* step to the **left** and then step back into the line—again using a gentle *light* step. Be sure to overemphasize the word *light* when asking students to do this. Once the first student steps back into the line, ask the next student in line to take a gentle *light* step to the **right** and then step back into the line—again using a gentle *light* step. The next student steps to the **left**, the next to the **right**—continue until all students have taken their gentle steps out of the line and back. Repeat several times to make sure all students have the basic idea.

Next, ask students to find a new place to stand in the line. This change of places is primarily so they realize a different idea is being introduced. To further clarify that this is a new idea, this time the activity starts from the *back* of the line.

This time, ask the first student to step toward the second, stopping just before they touch, and making lots of *sound* with his or her feet. As in the previous example, this time be sure to overemphasize the word *sound* when asking students to do this. The second student then steps away from the first student, toward the third student, stomping and making lots of *sound*—and so on down the line. After all students have done this several times, ask them to return to their seats.

Introduce students to the new vocabulary. The first demonstration was an example of a *transverse* wave—*in a transverse wave, as the wave is moving in one direction, it is creating a disturbance in a different direction.* Light waves are one example of a transverse wave. The second demonstration was an example of a *longitudinal* wave—*waves that have the same direction of vibration along their direction of travel.* Sound waves are one example of a longitudinal wave. Note that a longitudinal wave is also known as a *compression* wave, since certain points along the wave compress, much like an accordion.

Organize students into groups of three to four. Assign some of the groups to research transverse waves and others to research longitudinal waves using books or the Internet (if readily available). Each group has 10 minutes to do some basic research on their type of wave and report back on this question: *Was each demonstration an accurate representation of that type of wave? Why or why not?*

When all groups have reported back, clarify their learning by briefly elaborating on each type of wave. For example:

"Most kinds of waves are *transverse* waves. The most familiar visual example of this is a wave on the surface of water. As the wave travels in one direction, it is creating an up-and-down (*not* north-and-south) motion on the water's surface. And in scientific terms, *in a transverse wave, the particle displacement is perpendicular to the direction of wave propagation.*"

To clarify longitudinal waves . . .

"A wave in a Slinky is a good visualization of a longitudinal wave. All sound waves in the air are longitudinal waves. Or, in scientific terms, in a longitudinal wave, *the displacement of the medium is parallel to the propagation of the wave.*"

Articulate
–build in
time to
talk

The primary focus of this lesson is a basic understanding of the difference between the two types of waves, not a full understanding of the technical differences between them. However, these *scientific terms* are useful to introduce to students at this point, since they will reappear later in other lessons.

To truly remember the differences between these types of waves, students usually need multiple examples of each type of wave. Therefore, the first step is to repeat the original demonstrations. This time, however, only half of the students perform the demonstration while the other half watch; then they switch roles. Watching each type of wave being clearly modeled from a distance often helps students truly understand it. For further clarity, add words—for example, when modeling the longitudinal wave, students should loudly say the actual word, "Sound!" This will help them remember that a longitudinal wave is a sound wave.

Next, ask the students to return to their groups. Their task this time is to find a *different* way of demonstrating the wave they were researching to the rest of the class, using new props: Give the transverse groups the string or ribbons; give the longitudinal groups the Slinky toys.

These repeated and varied examples will help students clarify their understanding of the two primary types of waves and increase their ability to recall the types of waves later.

Phase Two

Near the end of the lesson, pose a series of reasoning-based questions to expand student thinking about different wave types. For example:

- In musical instruments, what happens when we change the frequency of the sound wave?

- Why is the size of a wave important to coastal erosion?

- How do dolphins use sound waves?

- Why do we see lightning before we see thunder?

- Is outer space quiet? Why?

- Can sound waves go around corners?

- Why does a pencil appear to be broken when placed in a glass of water?

- What is an echo?

Lesson 4

Contributing Teacher: Joel C. Palmer, Ed.D.

Subject: Physical Science

Lesson: Understanding Phases of Matter

Isolate—
identify the
core content

Key Concept	New Vocabulary
Understand the three states of matter (solid, liquid, gas) in terms of how the atoms are interconnected	Bonds Molecular energy Compression

Room setup: As much open space as possible (Go outside or use the gym if your classroom is too small.)

Music suggestions: *Like a Rock* by Bob Seger, *I Am a Rock* by Simon and Garfunkel, *Classical Gas* by Mason Williams, or *The Air That I Breathe* by The Hollies

Equipment: Books or Internet access to enable research into uses for compressed air and hydraulics

Translate –
choose the
engagement
strategy

Phase One

Games—Competition

Gather the students in a group in the middle of the room.

Announce that this lesson will begin with an activity. Explain that the activity will *not* make sense at first, but definitely will later. For now, students' only job is to participate and notice what people are doing.

Instruct students to grab hands with two different students.

Ask if anyone has formed a group of three. Tell them that this is not allowed. One side of the triangle must drop hands and link with other students so that the group is connected via a lattice of hands and arms.

Pick one student on the edge of the group and ask him to try to move to the other side of the group without anyone letting go of hands. Play music during the attempt. The task should prove difficult, if not impossible. Stop them before anyone gets hurt!

Now change the rules: The student can now let go of one hand at a time but must immediately grab the joined hands of two other people. This is the trigger for them to let go. One grabs the new person's hand while the other makes a grab for another set of joined hands, and the process repeats.

Practice in slow motion first and then ask the same student to once again attempt to move to the other side of the group. The idea is that the students will continuously change the hands they are holding, and the student will find it easy to move to the other side of the group.

After the student makes it to the other side, say, "Thank you. That was very well done. Everyone please let go." Say this as if the activity is over. Wait until students begin to move away from each other and then shout: "Freeze!"

When the students have stopped moving, ask them to look around and see what happened. Now they can return to their seats.

Discuss with the students what happened in the simulation.

Explain that the initial situation is analogous to a solid. The bonds in a solid are in place. They have no independent linear motion of translation because they are attached to one another. This was why the students could not drop hands. Explain that solids can have molecular energy as a result of vibration and rotation. This was demonstrated when the student tried to move to the other side. He or she could still move but couldn't move *out of place*. Point out that this is why solids have a definite shape and a definite volume. They cannot be *compressed*.

The second situation models a liquid, where the atoms or molecules are just as close to each other as in solids, but the materials can slip over each other to change places. This was modelled by the students constantly changing hands. Point out that this is why liquids have no shape, other than that of their container, but they do have a definite volume. In other words, a liquid won't expand to fill the whole container because it still has strong forces holding the particles close to each other. Explain that, like a solid, a liquid cannot be compressed under common pressures.

The last situation—when the students were moving away from each other—is like a gas. A gas is the most energetic phase of matter. The particles of gas, either atoms or molecules, have too much energy to settle down attached to each other or to come close to other particles to be attracted by them. Gas has no shape of its own—it will expand to fill the container as its particles continue to move away from each other. Explain that gas can be compressed.

In pairs or trios, students must now explain to each other the difference between the bonds in a solid, liquid, and gas. They must also remind each other which states have definite volumes and shapes and which can be compressed.

Split the class into three or four large groups. Tell them there will be a competition, and here are the rules:

The teacher will call out "Solid," "Liquid," or "Gas."

The first group to correctly replicate the molecular action called out gets a point.

The group with the most points at the end of 5 minutes gets a prize.

The teacher is the judge and his or her decision is final.

Play music after you call out each state to energize the activity.

The competition will embed strong kinesthetic memories.

Phase Two

To create a real-world connection, in groups, challenge students to use the research materials to find as many uses as possible for compressed air.

Finally, challenge students to explain why the hydraulic brake system in a car cannot work correctly if there is any air (gas) in the system.

GEOGRAPHY

Lesson 1

Contributing Teacher: N. R. Scozzi

Subject: Geography

Key Concept: Carrying Capacity

Key Concept	New Vocabulary
What determines a landscape's ability to support a number of people?	Carrying capacity Resource base Grasslands Temperate

Room setup: Normal seating; world biome map on the wall

Music suggestions: *Great Balls of Fire* by Jerry Lee Lewis, *Rubber Ball* by Bonnie Vee, or *Tossing and Turning* by The Ivy League

Equipment:
- Large bucket of tennis balls
- 3 students
- 3 letter signs: "D" desert, "G" grasslands, and "T" temperate (to be stuck on each student's back)
- 1 bucket or box
- Maps of a fictitious continent

Phase One

Props

With no explanation, nominate three students to have the letters stuck to their backs. In turn, they must stand and catch balls thrown by the teacher, with the following restrictions:

"D man" can only use one hand to catch and carry the balls

"G man" can use two hands to catch and carry the balls

"T man" can use both hands *and* use the box to store the balls

As soon as they drop a ball, their turn is over. Clearly "D man" can only catch and carry at most four balls; "G man" is likely to catch and carry more; while "T man" could seemingly go on forever.

Tell your students the balls are symbolic of people and the students symbolic of major landscapes. In small groups, ask them to identify "D man" (desert) and give reasons for its inability to carry many balls/people (lack of water).

Propose a change of circumstances: "What if 'D man' can now use two hands?" Lead a large-group discussion so students can grasp the idea of irrigation or piped-in water, for example in the desert areas of the western United States.

Continue the large-group discussion to identify "G man" and "T man." T is usually guessed as tropical but with Q & A, students work out that this is unlikely because of the degradation of soils very quickly after deforestation. Eventually, with reference to the world biome map, they suggest temperate areas.

The memory strategy here is incorporated within the activity, through the use of movement, engagement, a striking visual example, and, of course, laughter! Students can clearly recollect the activity, even to the extent that they remember which students were involved. The activity itself acts as the peg upon which the concept is hung.

Phase Two

To understand this concept more fully, ask students to analyze a hypothetical continent.

Organize students into groups of two to four. Give each group a large map of a fictitious continent.

Based on their understanding of the concept of carrying capacity, ask students to shade the areas of the map they believe are likely to have the highest population densities down to the areas of lowest population densities.

Finished maps are displayed at the front of the classroom, and a spokesman for each group outlines the reasons for the population density patterns they have chosen.

Lesson 2

Contributing Teacher: N. R. Scozzi

Subject: Geography

Key Concept: Urban Changes

Key Concept	New Vocabulary
What factors influence inner-city urban changes?	Urban decay Urban renewal Consolidation Gentrification Structural employment change

Room setup:	Tables arranged for small-group work. A sealed envelope on each station marked DO NOT OPEN UNTIL INSTRUCTED. A survivor reward poster outside the room and a small table placed outside the room for the Resource Bank.
Music suggestion:	*Survivor* theme song
Equipment:	• Several photos of housing (past and present), location maps, newspaper articles, and textbooks set on a table and referred to as a Resource Bank
	• Copies of the Resource Bank for each group
	• 2 sets of quiz questions in large envelopes for each group

Phase One

Games—TV

Outside the classroom, ask students to form groups of three or four. (This lesson begins outside the classroom door merely for the novelty effect—if you do not have sufficient space, the same activity could occur *in* your classroom.) Once they are in their groups, allow students to take a moment to study the Resource Bank. They can pick items up, if needed, for closer study. After two to three minutes, point out the For Rewards poster, and ask your students to read it carefully. Inform them that they will be able to pick up copies of all this

material in the classroom. When everyone has had an opportunity to review the For Rewards poster, dramatically open the classroom door and invite them inside so the challenge can begin!

Students enter the room with *Survivor* theme music playing. Each group takes a moment to collect their resources and find a table.

On each table is a sealed envelope containing the first quiz. It is clearly marked DO NOT OPEN UNTIL INSTRUCTED—building suspense.

Give each team 30 seconds to come up with a team name and write these on the board.

Introduce students to the new vocabulary they will need to understand the challenge in the envelope: *Urban decay, urban renewal, consolidation, gentrification,* and *structural employment change.* Students write these terms in their notes. For each term, provide a general definition and then an example. Ask each team to come up with one example to help illustrate the term, which they must add to their notes and present to the group.

Challenge students to come up with a doodle or an icon to represent each of the new vocabulary words, and draw this icon in the margin beside their notes. Tell students that when it's time to review, they will be able to recall the drawing, which will prompt a memory of the new vocabulary words and their definitions. Allow 3 minutes at most for this activity.

Now, instruct each group to open the envelope containing the first set of quiz questions. Groups must work together, using the resources, to complete the quiz. The quiz contains questions with prompts as to where students can find the answers in their resource bank. For example:

> *What is the target population for the area? (article)*
>
> *What density of population is suggested by photograph A?*
>
> *Name the main road running into the peninsula. (map)*
>
> *What is the definition of peninsula? (textbook)*
>
> *What has been challenging about redevelopment in the area? (article)*

When finished, teams take their answers to the teacher. If some answers are wrong, they are sent back to try again. Teams win by being first to arrive at the correct answers. Rather than teams being eliminated (as in the *Survivor* TV show), they receive points for their placing (10 points for first place, 7 for second place, and so on), which are written on the board.

When all teams have reached the correct answers, debrief the students by discussing the questions that caused the most problems.

Now tell students that they have another chance to win points. Teams pick up the second quiz envelope and the process repeats. The team with the biggest points total at the end wins a token prize.

Phase Two

Challenge students in pairs or trios to answer the following questions:

- Think about the towns you have lived in. Were they in a state of urban decay or renewal? What makes you think that?
- If your suburb became *gentrified*, what do you think would happen to the average family income in the area? What do you think would happen to the average family size in the area? Why do you think this?
- What would be the potential benefits and/or disadvantages to your family of housing consolidation in your area?

Lesson 3

Contributing Teacher: N. R. Scozzi

Subject: Geography (or Science)

Key Concept: Causes of Rainfall

Key Concept	New Vocabulary
What are the three main causes of the cooling of air and rainfall?	Humidity Lapse rate Frontal rain Convectional rain Relief rainfall

Room setup: Tables set up for small-group work

Music suggestions: *Raindrops Keep Falling on My Head* by Burt Bacharach and B. J. Thomas, *Laughter in the Rain* by Neil Sedaka, *Rhythm of the Rain* by The Cascades, or *Ain't No Mountain High Enough* by Marvin Gaye and Tammi Terrell

Equipment: • Story of Fred—one copy per group

• Graph/table of statistics (printed on the back of Fred's story)

• Weather charts (as shown below in the Criticate section)

Phase One

Story

The lesson starts with the teacher reading the following story. Students are told to sit back, relax, and listen—not to take notes.

Fred Climbs a Ridge

Fred loves to go hiking! Today he has decided to challenge himself and walk from the coast all the way up a local mountainside to the highest ridge top. Fred sets off as he normally does when he goes for a pleasant walk in the summer, wearing a T-shirt and carrying a long-sleeve sweater in his backpack should he need it along the way. It is fairly warm going along the valley floor, and he works up a bit of a sweat as he takes in the pleasant warm air, striding through the thick lowland forest.

After a while of walking up the ever-increasing incline, he finds that he has begun to shiver a little, so he puts on his sweater, thankful he had remembered to bring it along. While Fred is still enjoying his walk up the mountainside, he finds the visibility changes as he climbs—the higher he goes, the more he comes across misty conditions, and the air continues to grow cooler. Fred looks upward and is surprised to see even thicker clouds up above him and threatening rain showers skirting the ridges above.

Fred decides to turn back since he doesn't like the cold, and he certainly doesn't like getting wet. Indeed, as he looks back down the mountainside and out to sea he notices the wind picking up and banks of clouds rolling in. What a shame, since it had started out as such a nice day. "Ah well," he thinks to himself, "At least I suspected it might rain today, unlike last week when all that hot weather came to an abrupt end with those terrible afternoon downpours."

Ask students to form groups of two or three. Distribute a copy of the story of Fred to each group and have them review the story. The aim is for each person to know the basic sequence—what happens to Fred?—and the title of the story. Proceed only when all groups can state the title of the story and demonstrate they know the sequence.

Now, explain to students the key factors in the lesson. First, the title of the story introduces three of the five important factors they will need to know. "**F**red **C**limbs a **R**idge" provides the clue for the information within each first letter:

Fred = **F**rontal Rain

Climbs = **C**onvectional Rain

Ridge = **R**elief Rain

Explain each of these types of rain. For example, "The term *frontal rainfall* is derived from the fact that it occurs when two masses of air, one warm and the other cold, meet. This causes a 'front.' When the mass of warm air meets the mass of cold air, the warm air, which is lighter and less dense than the cold air, rises above the denser and heavier cold air mass. When the warm air is pushed upward, it cools. When air goes above the point of dew formation and is no longer able to hold all its water within, it begins to condense and form clouds. This leads to precipitation, and the rain can fall over a widespread geographical area."

Next, introduce the concepts of humidity and lapse rate. Although the basic idea of humidity will be familiar to most students, clarifying here with a specific definition—*the amount of water vapor in the air*—will help students clarify their statements later, when they are in the criticate phase of the lesson. Lapse rate—typically defined as *the rate of decrease with height for an atmospheric variable*—will often require a more in-depth explanation, and perhaps several examples.

In their groups, ask the students to discuss the following questions:

1. Why did Fred give up on his hike?

2. Can they see a correlation—a connection—between temperature and rainfall?

3. What if the wind changed direction?

Ask students first to recount as much of Fred's journey as possible, using the FCR acronym to help them. Next, ask them to look at their own life experiences—for example, mountain walks or snow skiing in winter—and see if they have had any similar experiences. Being able to recount the story of Fred's journey and their own life experiences should provide the mental triggers for the basic idea that the cooling of the air at higher altitudes increases the chance of rainfall. Finally, ask students to explain to each other in their groups the definitions for the five new vocabulary terms used in the lesson.

Phase Two

Exercise #1: Having a Fair Time in the United States!

Ask students to form groups of three of four. Each group is given two maps, one showing the United States in general, and another showing the next day's weather pattern. Groups are asked to use the maps to work out why the following happened:

- Charleston cancelled a city fair.

- Memphis applied to the Federal government for disaster relief.

- Central valley farmers in California were forecasting a jump in their harvest of fruit.

- The state of Wyoming was looking forward to a summer festival.

Exercise #2: Soccer Sojourn

Groups are now given two more maps, one showing Europe in general, and another one showing the predicated weather patterns for the next 3 days.

Groups are now told, "You have won tickets to Europe at the height of the European soccer season but you have to make a decision about which games you would like to watch. You can only visit *one* nation, so your choice is La Liga in Spain, The Premier league in England, or Series A in Italy. Don't forget that the games will be played over the next 24 hours, and you do not want to risk missing any games due to postponements!"

Groups complete a summary table giving their reasons why they might choose to visit or not to visit a particular country, based on their analysis of the weather map.

Lesson 4

Contributing Teacher: N. R. Scozzi

Subject: Geography

Key Concept: Relief Maps

Key Concept	New Vocabulary
Illustrating height on a map	Compass point directions Contour interval Contour lines Steepness of slope

Room setup: Tables for small-group work; teacher wears a pirate hat and eye patch.

Music suggestions: *A Pirate Looks at 40* by Jimmy Buffett, *Coast of High Barbary* by Joseph Arthur, or *Island Girl* by Elton John

Equipment:
- Scrolls with pirate story for each group of students
- Base map for each group
- 3 colored cardboard cutouts of three elevations for each group

Phase One

Story

As students enter the classroom, ask them to sit together in groups of three or four. Each group nominates a captain.

Option A (for confident actors): Adopt a Caribbean accent and read the pirate story as it appears on the scroll. Use hand gestures to reinforce the underlying concepts being introduced.

Option B: Give out the scroll to each group, and instruct the captain to read the story to his or her team.

Ask each captain to send a delegate to the front of the room to collect supplies for the activity. These supplies include the base map of the island, three pieces of land area, and the scroll (if not already given out in Option B):

(Spoken with a pirate accent, using large hand gestures!)

"Ooh arr Me Arties !"

Many years ago a pirate ship was travelling north, when it became lost at sea. After several days of wandering aimlessly, the lookout spotted an island.

As it neared the island, the lookout saw a small bay on the southern coast with a natural harbor. The pirates dropped anchor and set about exploring the green landscape. However, they soon realized there wasn't anything interesting at this level. So, they looked up above the 10m height to an area of light brown landscape covered in pretty red flowers. They decided to explore it.

The land at the 10m height offered quite a good view over the bay. Again, though, the pirates discovered this area held nothing of interest to them either. Yet, glancing up another 10m they noticed the land looked quite different again and they thought they might find something of interest up there—or at least get a better view around the island.

So they climbed up to the 20m height and found this level of the island was covered with dark brown rocks. One of the sailors even climbed to the very top of the island and at the height of 30m had a great view of the green land at the coast that rose to 10m, the light brown landscape and pretty red flowers between 10 & 20m, and the brown rocky landscape above the 20m height. The north coast of the island, he noticed, was quite steep. But in the end there was no treasure to be found on this island, so they went back to their ship and sailed away …

Base map:

Three land-area pieces:

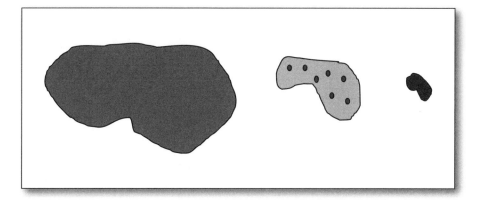

Challenge teams to construct the island from the story by setting the land area pieces in approximately the correct places. At the north (top) side of the island, the pieces should all be quite near each other, showing the steepness of the cliff. At this point the teacher should introduce the vocabulary term *steepness of slope*—where the lines of the different areas are quite close together.

Next, with the teacher's guidance—and using this model as a starting point—each group of students works together to create a map of the island on a large sheet of blank paper. They begin by drawing an outline of the island. Next, they add the smaller 10-meter height area, the even smaller 20-meter area, and finally the top of the island at 30 meters.

Once the maps are finished, introduce the vocabulary term *contour lines*—the border around the different elevations. Students write in the height of the area near the border at its maximum height—for example, the coastline at 0 meters, and then the 10-meter and 20-meter areas. Explain that these different elevations are called *contour areas*, and they have both shape and height. Students then lightly color in the various contour areas of the map with the appropriate colors, as described in the pirate story.

Finally, ask students to create a key or legend to their map, showing the height at each part of the island. They must also add the compass point directions as well.

When all maps are complete, the teacher explains that this type of map is called a *relief map*, meaning one that shows the various elevations in an area of land. Students are now invited to view the maps created by other groups, noting differences and similarities between those they created and those of other groups.

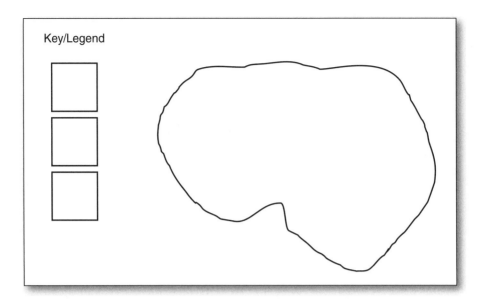

Key/Legend

Several memory strategies are incorporated into this lesson and can be revisited later with ease to reinforce the lesson.

- Stories are easy to remember. To help students recall the key concepts, in subsequent lessons invite them to find a partner and retell the story. Then have the pair quickly sketch the island map again and ask them to point out the contour lines and contour areas.

- The use of the pirate accent—even (or especially?) if done badly—brings novelty and laughter to the lesson, making it immediately more memorable. When students retell the story, invite them to use an accent!

- The use of large hand gestures when the teacher first tells the story to indicate changes in the topography is a key part of the recall for some students. When students retell the story, invite them to use hand gestures as well.

Phase Two

Challenge students to answer the following questions in their groups. Answers must be substantiated by a line of reasoning using the new vocabulary:

- How did you show that the north coast was steeper than the south of the island?

- How might a very gentle slope be shown on a map?

- Where would you choose to build a home or farm crops on the island and why?

- Where would you find the most exciting rock climbing?

- Name some professions where your ability to read a relief map could be useful or even save your life.

- You have been scuba diving for too long and must avoid elevations of more than 5,000 ft. Use a map to find a safe route to drive from one city to another.

BUSINESS STUDIES

Lesson 1

Teacher: Natasha Terry-Armstrong

Subject: Commerce

Lesson: Reasons for Rules and Laws

Isolate – identify the core content

Key Concept	New Vocabulary
To understand and explain the need for laws in society	Anarchy Legislation Enforcement Sanctions

Room setup: Tables for small-group work. The teacher wears a hat or scarf to denote airline cabin crew. Display an ocean/desert island image on a poster or on-screen.

Music suggestions: *I Fought the Law* by The Bobby Fuller Four, *Island Boy* by Kenny Chesney, or *I Will Live on Islands* by Josh Rouse

Translate – choose the engagement strategy

Phase One

Story

As students enter the classroom, your commentary makes it clear the class is pretending to board a flight: *"Ladies and gentlemen, please take your seats as quickly as you can and fasten your seatbelts for take-off."*

Narrate the process of getting air bound, but then first one engine fails and then the other . . . students adopt the brace position . . . and the plane crashes into the ocean.

This sets the scene—reinforced by your visuals.

Tell your students they are the only survivors on a deserted island with no belongings except the clothes they are wearing. What will they do?

Articulate – build in time to talk

At their tables, students brainstorm and discuss what they would do. Play tropical island music during the discussion. Support the discussion by putting up the follow questions on the board:

- What are your priorities? (water, shelter, food)
- What tasks need to be done? Who will do them?
- Who decides which tasks get done first?
- What if the person does not complete the task?
- Who coordinates the tasks (who is the leader)? How is the leader chosen? What if there is no consensus on the leader chosen?

Teams present their ideas to the class. While debriefing their decisions, introduce the new vocabulary (anarchy, legislation, enforcement, sanctions). Lead students to the understanding that they have started to create rules on their desert island.

The process of self-discovery, assisted by group discussion, creates strong memories of the key concepts. Reinforce students' memories by asking them to create *mind maps* of the concepts they have discussed, using the new vocabulary.

Phase Two

In pairs, or individually, students complete the following table to help them identify the importance of having laws in society and reflect on their own beliefs, standards, and values.

	Island	Society
Why are rules necessary?		
Are some rules more important than others? Why?		
Who makes the rules?		
How are the rules enforced?		
Are the rules followed by everyone? Why? Why not?		
What process is used to ensure that the rules are fair?		

Lesson 2

Teacher: Natasha Terry-Armstrong

Subject: Business Studies/Economics

Lesson: Circular Flow of Income

Key Concept	New Vocabulary
To understand the circular flow of income in the economy and how this is managed through economic policy	Leakages Injections Circular flow Monetary policy Interest rates Recession Inflation

Room setup: Normal seating

Music suggestions: *Money, Money, Money* by ABBA, *If Money Talks* by Jason & the Scorchers, or *Spending Money* by Jimmy Buffet

Equipment:
- 5 laminated signs containing images and/or words to represent Households, Firms, Financial Sector, Government Sector, and International Sector

- 8 laminated images with dollar signs to represent money, carrying the words Wages, Consumer Spending, Saving, Investment, Taxes, Government Spending, Import, and Export

- Template of the circular flow of money diagram—one complete for the board/screen and one for each student with labels missing

Phase One

Props

Introduce the idea that income flows through the economy.

Ask two students to stand at either side of the room at the front (mirroring their position on your template diagram), holding the Households and Firms signs.

Ask students to discuss with a partner *how* the money makes its way between the Households and Firms. After a few minutes, open the floor for their ideas. Prompt toward buying goods (Consumer

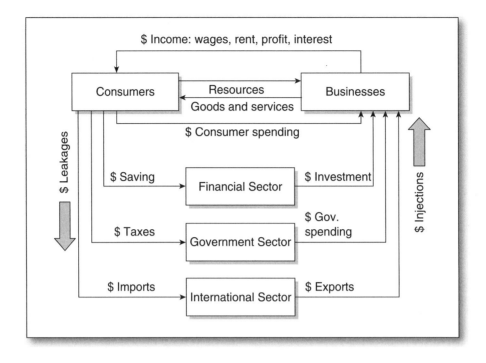

Spending) and wages. Give the students who suggested these ideas the appropriate sign and ask them to walk between the Household and Firms signs in a circular pattern.

Suggest that households do not spend every dollar earned on goods and services.

Gather ideas as to where else the income might flow: taxation to government; savings into the financial sector; purchasing imported goods to the international sector.

Give the sector sign to the student who suggested it, and get that student to stand in the same position as on the diagram.

For each sector, discuss what the money flow would be called—for example, taxes—and give out the appropriate money signs. Ask students with money signs to walk the correct path—for example, "Taxes" walks between "Households" and "Government."

Introduce and reinforce the new vocabulary during the discussion.

Thank student sign holders and ask them to sit down.

Put up the circular flow of money diagram and ask students if they recognize it. Take down the visual.

Give each student a template for the circular flow of income diagram with missing labels. Ask students to complete the template.

Collect the templates. Now ask students to draw the diagram on their own.

In pairs, students help each other to fill in any gaps. Pairs find other pairs to help them, and so on, until everyone has completed the diagram.

Phase Two

Ask small groups of students to consider the logical relationship between the ideas just discussed. What happens to the diagram when

- The Reserve Bank raises interest rates?
- The Government gives all citizens $900 as part of the economic stimulus package?
- There is high unemployment in the economy?
- There is strong economic growth?

Lesson 3

Teacher: Natasha Terry-Armstrong

Subject: Business Studies

Lesson: Drivers of Globalization

Key Concept	New Vocabulary
The key drivers of the process of globalization	Transnational corporations Deregulation Trade liberalization Protectionism

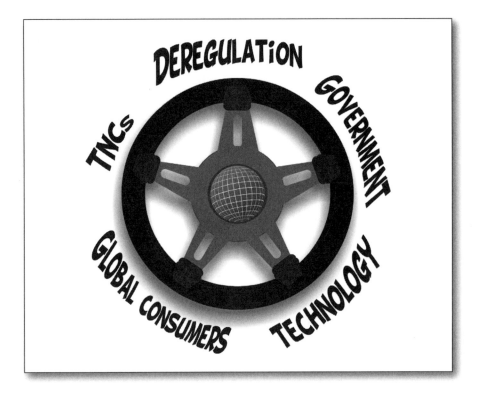

Room setup:	Tables for group work
Music suggestions:	*Who's Going to Drive You Home?* by The Cars, *Big Money* by Garth Brooks, or *Money for Nothing* by Dire Straits
Equipment:	• A steering wheel
	• Prizes for the winning team
	• Blank signs

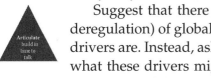

Phase One

Props

As students enter the room, walk around holding a steering wheel making terrible puns: "I'm going to drive you mad this lesson," or "We are steering into a new topic today."

Finally, put your students out of their misery by explaining that today they will be learning about the drivers of globalization.

Suggest that there are many "drivers" (for example, technology, deregulation) of globalization, but don't tell your students what these drivers are. Instead, ask them to talk to the people around them about what these drivers might be. Next, ask for ideas. Each student who names one of the drivers you are looking for writes it on a sign and stands with it at the front of the room.

Prompt the discussion until you get all the drivers you're looking for: transnational corporations, global consumers, impact of technology, role of government, and deregulation of financial markets.

Split the rest of the class into teams around each driver. Challenge the teams to provide at least three examples of how their driver strengthens globalization. The team with the most examples wins a prize.

The memory strategy here is incorporated within the activity. Students clearly recollect the activity, even to the extent of recalling the name of the student holding each driver. The students themselves act as the pegs upon which the concept is hung.

Phase Two

Staying in their groups, students are now asked to brainstorm the positive and negative aspects of their driver, decide whether on balance the result is good or bad, and justify their conclusions back to the class. This helps students to understand the power of globalization, consider alternative perspectives of how it might be viewed by different stakeholders, and reflect on where globalization fits in their personal value system.

Lesson 4

Contributing Teacher: Natasha Terry-Armstrong

Subject: Business Studies

Lesson: Business Life Cycle

Key Concept	New Vocabulary
Each business goes through the stages of the business life cycle with identifiable characteristics	Establishment Growth Maturity Postmaturity (decline, renewal, steady state) Market share

Room setup:	Normal seating
Music suggestions:	*Curve* by Tim Hanauer, *Puzzle* by Dada, *Takin' Care of Business* by Bachman-Turner Overdrive, or *Business as Usual* by The Eagles
Equipment:	• Life Cycle: Four Basic Stages diagram for each student cut into nine jigsaw pieces and sorted by piece—that is, create piles of identical pieces • Flip chart paper

Phase One

Games—Jigsaw

On entering the classroom, each student receives a pile of identical jigsaw pieces. Students are challenged to find the nine different pieces by swapping with their classmates. When they have all nine pieces, they are to return to their seats and complete the jigsaw. Prizes will be given to the first students to assemble the jigsaw correctly. Music plays loudly during the ensuing scramble. Finally, students stick their assembled diagrams into workbooks.

The teacher leads a group discussion, with the complete diagram on display, about the stages of the business life cycle—introducing the new vocabulary. At the end, students in pairs or trios take turns explaining the different stages to each other. Those explaining cannot look at their diagrams. Their partners can prompt them if they get stuck.

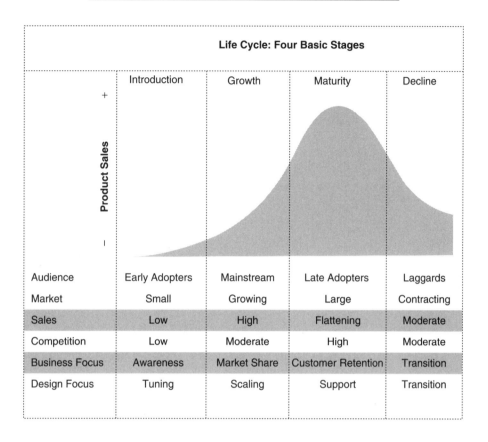

Life Cycle: Four Basic Stages

	Introduction	Growth	Maturity	Decline
Audience	Early Adopters	Mainstream	Late Adopters	Laggards
Market	Small	Growing	Large	Contracting
Sales	Low	High	Flattening	Moderate
Competition	Low	Moderate	High	Moderate
Business Focus	Awareness	Market Share	Customer Retention	Transition
Design Focus	Tuning	Scaling	Support	Transition

Challenge the pairs or trios to re-create the business life cycle diagram from memory on large pieces of flip chart paper. If some teams are struggling after a few minutes, groups are allowed to "cheat"—they are given 30 seconds to send a runner to see another group's diagram to figure out what they've forgotten. Finally, groups are challenged to review other teams' diagrams. If they can find a mistake or an omission, they are allowed to correct it in red pen.

Phase Two

To help students understand the relevance of the diagram, ask them in groups to brainstorm at least two possible challenges for businesses at each stage of the business life cycle and strategies that could be used to deal with these challenges.

As each group presents their ideas, the larger group is challenged to find real business examples of companies that have faced these challenges. The teacher leads a broader discussion of what those companies did and how well their strategies worked.

5

Putting Power Into the Delivery

The Keys to Managing a Green Light Classroom

Implementing the ideas in this book may require you to introduce new elements into your classroom. For example, the lessons in the previous chapter come with suggestions for memory strategies, music, and room setup. They also require you to facilitate frequent student conversations. Recognizing that, for some teachers, these will be quite profound changes, this chapter takes a more detailed look at four fundamental techniques for making engaging lessons more effective:

1. **Recall:** teaching your students memory pegs

2. **Rock:** using music to support activities and learning

3. **Reorganize:** matching your classroom setup to your lesson

4. **Reflect:** setting up productive student conversations

Teaching your students memory pegs is important since it demonstrates the power of using memory strategies and provides students who find recall difficult with an amazing tool for review. The other three issues are important to consider for almost any lesson, in any content area. They are powerful teaching techniques that make the difference between an activity limping slowly forward, or bounding toward success.

1. Recall: Teaching Your Students Memory Pegs

Memory pegs were mentioned under the heading "Replicate" on page 28 in Chapter 2 and used in English lesson 3 on page 86. They are important because they offer any student an easy way to remember information. Memory pegs are based on the way the mind works. They don't require you to be smart or to have a good memory. Anyone can use them to extraordinary effect, but first you have to embed them in your memory.

Here they are:

The Peg	The Action
1. Sun	Make a circle with your hands
2. Eyes	Bring two fingers to your eyes
3. Triangle	Draw a triangle in the air with your fingers
4. Stove	Touch all four burners on a stove
5. Fingers	Hold up the five fingers of one hand
6. Sticks	Pick up sticks from the ground
7. 7-Up	Take a big drink from a can of 7-Up
8. Octopus	Put your arms out like an octopus
9. Line	Draw a line in the air in front of you
10. Hen	Flap your arms like a chicken's wings
11. Fence	Two fingers in the air, and make a series of fence posts
12. Eggs	Crack an imaginary egg
13. Black Cat	Pet the cat
14. Heart	Make a heart in the air in front of you with your fingers
15. Fame	Arms spread wide, say "Fame!"
16. Driving	Drive an imaginary car
17. Magazine	Turn the pages of an imaginary magazine
18. Vote	Make a check mark in the air
19. TV Remote	Click the imaginary remote at the TV
20. 20-20 Vision	Make circles with your hands around your eyes

Step 1: Learning the Pegs Yourself!

Before you can share them with your students, you need to know how to use the pegs yourself. Learn them by first saying the number, then saying the peg associated with that number, while doing the motion. For example, to learn the first peg, out loud say, "One—sun." At the same time, do the action of making a circle with your hands in the air in front of you. Next, say, "Two—eyes." At the same time, do the action of bringing two fingers toward your eyes, pointing at them. Continue in this way until you feel confident you've learned all 20 of the pegs.

To verify that you really can remember them, try several things. First, give a friend the list of the 20 pegs to test you while you go through them in order. Remember—*always say the number, then say the name of the peg as you do the action.* Next, try doing the 20 pegs backward, starting at 20, and going down to 1. Again, ask your friend to make sure you get them all correct. Finally, ask your friend to call out random numbers between 1 and 20, and you tell your friend the peg while doing the action.

When you are confident you know the 20 pegs, you're ready to use them.

Step 2: Using the Pegs Yourself

Here's how to use the pegs at a very basic level. Begin by making a random list of 20 common household objects. We've filled in the first few, just to get you started, so please fill in the rest of the list. *Be sure to do this before you read on!*

1.	book	11.	
2.	refrigerator	12.	
3.	lamp	13.	
4.		14.	
5.		15.	
6.		16.	
7.		17.	
8.		18.	
9.		19.	
10.		20.	

The next step is to use the pegs to memorize this list. The words you've learned, connected to each number, can be used like mental pegs. You can hang a picture of the thing you want to remember onto the picture that's already in your head at each number. Here's how it works.

Take the first thing on this list you want to remember. How do you remember it's a book? You start by thinking of the peg you've learned for number one. Remember? It's the sun, and the motion is making a circle in front of you like a sun. The key is to *take the motion you already know—making a circle—start making it again, but then let it change into a motion that might remind you of a book.*

For example, you might start making the circle but then square it off and say the word "book." Starting the motion you already learned becomes the trigger for the motion, which changes into a specific motion that triggers the memory. Try it right now. Do it in the air in front of you—start making a circle, then change it into a square, and say, "One—book." Remember, it's important to keep saying the number!

Let's try another one. The second one on this list is a refrigerator. First, start making the motion for the second peg. Remember, the second peg is eyes and the motion is your two fingers coming toward your eyes. Now, start that motion, but change it into something that will trigger a memory of a refrigerator. It could be anything that *you* want to make up, but for now, let's imagine that your fingers start coming toward your eyes, and then you bend them into hooks, which you use to open the refrigerator door, as you say, "Two—refrigerator." Try that right now. Do it several times.

For the third one, use the same idea—start with the action you know for that peg, and change it into something that will trigger a memory of the item on the list. Can you make one up right now, before you read on? TRY IT! Perhaps, since the third peg is a triangle and the motion is to make a triangle with your fingers, you could start making the triangle, but as your fingers come down, pull on an imaginary lamp cord, and say, "Three—lamp."

Now, continue memorizing the list you created, using this approach. For each item, start the motion of the peg you already know, and then change it to become a motion that triggers the memory of the item on the list. Do this for each one several times, always saying the number and the item as you do the motion. Continue down the list until you've done all 20. Finally, grab a sheet of paper and write down the 20 things on that list!

If you're like most people, you'll get most of them—perhaps all of them—right away! To make sure you have the hang of using the memory pegs, you might want to repeat this process several times, each time using a new list. Only do it once a day, at most. When you're confident you understand how the process works, you're ready to introduce this technique to your students.

Step 3: Demonstrating the Pegs to Your Students

Here's one way to introduce your students to the pegs. Done properly, it's completely amazing to your students—and enormously empowering. For many students, this will be the first time they have ever managed to easily remember information.

First, ask your students to call out 20 household items, and get a couple of volunteers to write them on the board. Don't tell them why you're doing it; just ask them to give suggestions while you write them up. When you have 20 things written on the board, tell the students you'll come back to these later, and get them busy doing some type of activity where they are working with each other. While they're busy, use the peg strategy to memorize the list. Don't be too obvious about your hand motions, and take as much time as you need.

When you feel you have the list memorized, you can start. Tell your students you're going to memorize the list. Ask them to time 20 seconds for you. When they say go, turn your back on them and look at the 20 things on the board—use this time to check once again that you DO know them! Then, turn around, and without looking at the board, start saying the items, in order. They'll be staring at you, amazed! And then, if you're feeling confident, ask them to call out random numbers, such as "7" or "15," and show that you can remember any of the items from the list, even when called out at random.

Now that you've got their attention, tell them that—by the end of the lesson—they will also be able to perform this amazing feat of memory.

Step 4: Teaching the Pegs to the Students

Teaching the pegs to the students follows the same sequence that you used when you were learning them yourself:

- Explain that for them to do this, they must first learn some pegs. Make it clear why they are called pegs, using the explanation from this section.

- Teach the 20 pegs to the students as a group, going in order and asking them to repeat each one, always doing the actions.

- Next, students practice the pegs in pairs, or trios, doing them first in order, then backward, then testing each other at random.

- Demonstrate how you used the motion of each peg to make a connection to the list of items on the board. Do the first few with them, and then get them to work together to memorize the rest of the list. Give them 5 minutes at most!

- After the 5 minutes are over, erase the items from the board! Ask your students to work together to write down the 20 items from the board. Celebrate their success!

When students have proven to themselves that they can memorize 20 individual items this way, you're ready for the final step.

Step 5: Using the Pegs to Learn Content

The final piece in understanding the memory pegs is to have students apply them to remembering content they need to learn. Interestingly, once the basic idea is in place, this last part is surprisingly simple, yet incredibly powerful.

The key is to isolate the important points from any unit or lesson. Write these points on the board. For example, if your students are doing a history unit, on the day before the test, write up the 20 most important facts, such as names, dates, or locations. Give students time to work together and use the pegs to memorize them. When students can remember these keys points, they'll easily be able to recall other information *related* to these central points.

Can students remember multiple lists? Yes, they can! The pegs can be used to remember key points from several different content areas if necessary. Try them in various ways, with various subject areas, and watch how flexible, adaptable, and *useful* these memory pegs can be.

II. Rock: Using Music to Support Activities and Learning

Used correctly, music can unleash your students' energy and help guide them in a useful direction. Just as important, when you use music in the classroom, you will expend less of your own valuable energy (Burko & Elliot, 1997; Jensen, 1996). For example, music is a mood enhancer. With no effort from the teacher—other than hitting "play"—music will calm and cheer students who arrive stressed or grumpy. It will motivate reluctant participants and engage even the coolest nonconformer.

Although educators have been aware of the power of music for many years, the cost and effort of playing music in the classroom used to be prohibitive. However, with the advent of digital music, iPods, and low-cost speakers, every classroom can now have a sound track.

Here are five keys places where music will help to support the lessons in this book:

1. Music as a signal

2. Music during movement

3. Music matching a theme

4. Music behind small-group discussions

5. Music after class

Music as a Signal

Music is a wonderful means of getting your students' attention. Rather than raising your voice, all you have to do is raise the volume of your music. Here's how it works: Whenever you want to quiet the class, simply turn up the volume above the noise level in the room, and then cut the music off. The sudden drop in volume will cause students to stop talking and turn to look at you. All you have to do is talk into the silence.

Use music in this way to signal

- The class is starting
- It's time to pause to hear another instruction
- It's time to move to the next station
- A group discussion is over
- An activity is over

Music During Movement

Whenever your students are moving, use music to motivate them to accomplish the task more rapidly (Jensen, 2000). This works for longer periods of movement, for example, when students are rearranging tables and chairs. It also works for 20- or 30-second bursts of movement, for example, when students are forming groups or moving to get supplies.

Upbeat, bright, energetic music is best in these situations. Since our goal is to move students rapidly to the next direction or activity, music provides an auditory stimulus to get them moving! This saves us from having to expend our own precious energy to get our students up and motivated.

Music to Match a Theme

You may have noticed that the music suggestions in the lessons are themed to the activity. You don't have to use themed music throughout your whole lesson—in fact, it will become annoying if you do. However, playing one themed song to match your translation technique will support engagement and recall, especially for your auditory students.

It doesn't matter if the connection is corny or tenuous; for many students, the moment they heard *I Feel the Earth Move Under My Feet* by Carole King, on the day you taught earthquakes, will be their memory hook for the lesson. Google will help you find many song ideas, but for the definitive list, *The Green Book of Songs* (Green, 2005) is a dictionary of songs by topic. This astonishing resource is now available online at www.greenbookofsongs.com.

Music Behind Small-Group Discussions

Whenever you introduce small-group discussions, there is a chance that conversation from one group may intrude on another. By playing music lightly in the background, you can lessen this sense of interference.

This effect is called a musical *pad*. Physical padding is used to soundproof rooms in a home, walls in an apartment building, or a music studio. In the classroom, using light background music effectively pads the room so sound from one group will not interfere with sound from another group. In a silent room, if one group breaks into laughter, the sudden intrusion of sound can be quite disruptive to other conversations. However, a pad of music reduces the effect of the interruption.

This pad can also *encourage* conversation within a group. In a silent room, it may be a bit intimidating for some students to speak up and voice their opinions—even in a very small group. With protection and privacy created by a music pad, even timid students feel free to engage themselves in the discussion.

Since students will be talking during this time, be careful of using songs with well-known lyrics. You want students talking to each other—not singing along!

Music After Class

You can use ending music to create a positive feeling that students will take away from your classroom. This will frequently be the first thing they think about when they begin to organize their thoughts for their next class with you. Try using *Celebration* by Kool and the Gang to create an upbeat mood, or leave them laughing with *Hit the Road Jack* by Ray Charles.

III. Reorganize: Matching Your Classroom Setup to Your Lesson

Dynamic lessons often require a different room setup. It is well worth the time and effort to make sure your classroom is physically set up to match the activity. Some options follow.

Debate:

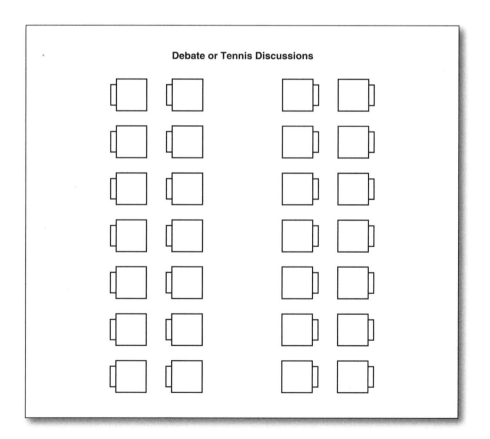

Debate or Tennis Discussions

Groups:

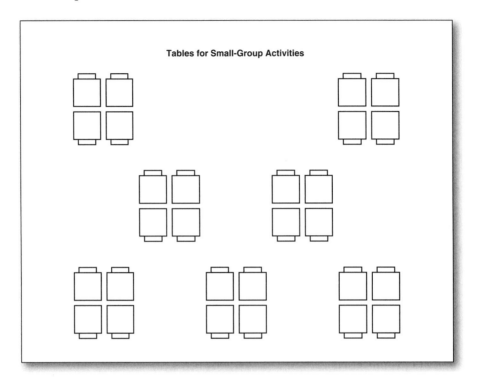

U-shape, center of the room left open for activities:

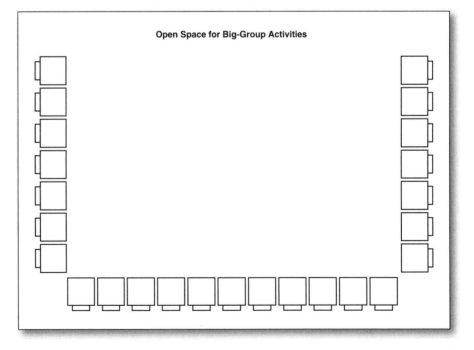

Wherever possible, employ your *students* to arrange the room for the activity! This offers the multiple benefits of

- Reducing your time and effort needed for the setup.
- Introducing student movement, which gets the blood flowing and activates the brain.
- Alerting students that something new is coming.
- Setting the *mood* for the lesson, allowing that you play upbeat music while they work.
- Giving students a higher sense of ownership of their classroom experience.

IV. Reflect: Setting Up Productive Student Conversations

The lessons in this book rely heavily on students discussing topics in small and large groups. Here are two simple techniques to help you set up and facilitate these conversations.

Getting Helpful Responses in a Large-Group Discussion

When asking questions of the large group, always allow students a short period of time to organize their thoughts and prepare their responses. You can do this either by encouraging them to talk to each other about their ideas or by giving them a moment to review their notes and write down some possible answers. Giving students a few moments to think, process, and practice their responses will dramatically improve the quality of the ensuing discussion.

One of the side benefits of using this technique is that allowing all students the opportunity to talk or reflect, even briefly, gives each person the time to process the information in a different mode than passive listening. And when students process information *actively*, even for a short period, they are more likely to remember the content. This is true even for those students who do *not* talk during the ensuing discussion.

How to Set Up Small-Group Discussions

Use the following Question-Clarify-Question sequence to set up small-group discussions:

First

Ask the general question so that students can see the overall picture.

Second

Provide details that clarify the question so that students understand the type of responses you expect.

Third

Repeat the original question—usually slightly rephrased—to serve as a springboard for the group to jump into the general discussion.

For example, a history teacher might say, "(1) In your groups, discuss what you think were some of the most significant factors that resulted in the Great Depression of the 1930s. (2) For example, do you think it was primarily overspending by the public, or was it a sudden lack of jobs, or the government's failure to provide sufficient regulation of certain industries in the preceding years? (3) So, turn to your team: What do you think were some of the most significant causes of the Great Depression? Begin!" *Music plays to signal the start of the discussion.*

Without this clear, linear setup, student conversations will often be hesitant, vague, or accidentally off-purpose. However, using this three-step sequence will guide students in your intended direction and help them to rapidly engage in the conversation.

Authors' Final Note

You don't have to see the whole staircase, just take the first step.

—Martin Luther King

As authors, we cherish a fond fantasy that teachers will read this book and immediately change many aspects of their lessons, coming up with creative translation activities; letting students talk more; using memory strategies in every lesson; and prompting and modeling critical thinking.

However, we are also well aware of the extreme challenges facing high school educators. Many secondary teachers do not have their own classrooms. Others battle serious, and often frightening, behavioral issues. Most are responsible for many additional activities beyond their own curriculum. Few have enough preparation time. Under these circumstances, we know that making the time and effort to change your teaching strategies seems overwhelming, *even if you can see the possibilities in changing your approach.* As secondary teachers ourselves, we both fully understand the yawning chasm between thinking "That's a good idea" and actually going through the pain of doing something different.

Therefore, our more realistic hope for you, our reader, is simply this:

Act on what makes sense to you.

In other words, if, when you were reading this book and the sample lessons it contains, something struck you as a potentially useful idea, that's where you should begin. Rather than attempting to make multiple, simultaneous changes to your teaching style, it might be good to begin by doing something as simple as adjusting the physical arrangement of your classroom, with the goal of prompting more student interaction. Or you might add a very deliberate memory strategy into those topics that, in the past, your students have struggled to understand. Or you could include one or two critical thinking questions in your lessons each week.

Act on what makes sense to you, and watch to see if these small changes bear fruit. Are your students learning new material faster, remembering it longer, and performing better on tests? Are they more engaged in your classroom? Are they thinking more deeply about your content?

Once you see one strategy working, perhaps you'll be inspired to come back and choose another one to try out. In this way, over time—even in the complex, convoluted, and challenging world of secondary teaching—you really *can* create positive, valuable, and lasting change in your classroom. Taking that first small step forward can lead you rapidly—perhaps much more rapidly than you thought—toward becoming a Green Light teacher, making your classroom an even more successful learning environment.

Whether your journey toward Green Light teaching starts with one small step or a dramatic leap three at a time up the staircase, we'd be delighted to hear about your experience. Please send any Green Light stories to rich@drrichallen.com.

References

Allen, R. (2008). *Green light classrooms: Teaching techniques that accelerate learning*. Thousand Oaks, CA: Corwin.

Allen, R. (2010). *High-impact teaching strategies for the "XYZ" era of education*. Boston, MA: Allyn & Bacon.

Ausubel, D. P. (1967). *Learning theory and classroom practice* [Bulletin No. 1]. Toronto: The Ontario Institute for Studies in Education.

Bartlett, F. (1932). *Remembering*. Cambridge, UK: Cambridge University Press.

Burko, H., & Elliot, R. (1997). Hands-on pedagogy vs. hands-off accountability. *Phi Delta Kappan, 80*(5), 394–400.

Clark, A. C. (1973). Hazards of prophecy: The failure of imagination. In *Profiles of the future: An enquiry into the limits of the possible* (Rev ed., pp. 14, 21, 36). Ventura, CA: Bantam Books.

Costa, A. (2008). The thought-filled curriculum. *Educational Leadership, 65*(5), 20–24.

Education Bureau. (2002). *Basic education curriculum guide*. Wan Chai, Hong Kong: Author.

Epstein, A. (2008). An early start on thinking. *Educational Leadership, 65*(5), 38–42.

Garner, B. K. (2007). *Getting to got it! Helping struggling students learn how to learn*. Alexandria, VA: Association for Supervision and Curriculum Development.

Green, J. (2005). *The Green book of songs by subject: The thematic guide to popular music* (5th ed.). Nashville, TN: Professional Desk References.

Head, H. (1920). *Studies in neurology*. New York, NY: Oxford University Press.

Jensen, E. (1996). *Brain-based learning*. Del Mar, CA: Turning Point Publishing.

Jensen, E. (2000). *Music with the brain in mind*. San Diego, CA: The Brain Store.

Jensen, E. (2001). *Arts with the brain in mind*. Alexandria, VA: Association for Supervision and Curriculum Development.

Jensen, E. (2005). *Teaching with the brain in mind* (2nd ed.). Alexandria, VA: Association for Supervision and Curriculum Development.

Kagan, S. (2000). *Silly sports and goofy games*. San Clemente, CA: Kagan Publishing.

Kagan, S., & Kagan, M. (2009). *Kagan cooperative learning*. San Clemente, CA: Kagan Publishing.

Kirsch, I. (1999). The response expectancy: An introduction. In I. Kirsch (Ed.), *How expectancies shape experiences* (p. 7). Washington, DC: American Psychological Association.

Marzano, R. J. (2007). *The art and science of teaching: A comprehensive framework for effective instruction.* Alexandria, VA: Association for Supervision and Curriculum Development.

Marzano, R. J. (2009). Teaching with interactive whiteboards. *Educational Leadership, 67*(3), 80–82.

Marzano, R. J., & Haystead, M. (2009). *Final report on the evaluation of the Promethean technology.* Englewood, CO: Marzano Research Laboratory.

Nichols, S. L., & Berliner, D. C. (2008). Testing the joy out of learning. *Educational Leadership, 65*(6), 14–18.

Piaget, J. (1926). *The language and thought of the child.* New York, NY: Harcourt, Brace.

Slavin, R. E. (1988). *Educational psychology: Theory into practice.* Englewood Cliffs, NJ: Prentice Hall.

Sprenger, M. (2009). Focusing the digital brain. *Educational Leadership, 67*(1), 34–39.

Swartz, R. (2008). Energizing learning. *Educational Leadership, 65*(5), 26–31.

Tulving, E. (1984). Precis of elements of episodic memory. *Behavioural and Brain Sciences, 7,* 223–268.

U.S. Department of Education. (2010). *Under Secretary Martha Kanter's remarks at the Association of American Colleges and Universities annual meeting.* Retrieved from http://www.ed.gov/news/speeches/under-secretary-martha-kanters-remarks-association-american-colleges-and-universities

Wiggins, G., & McTighe, J. (2008). Put understanding first. *Educational Leadership, 65*(8), 36–41.

Index

CORWIN
A SAGE Company

The Corwin logo—a raven striding across an open book—represents the union of courage and learning. Corwin is committed to improving education for all learners by publishing books and other professional development resources for those serving the field of PreK–12 education. By providing practical, hands-on materials, Corwin continues to carry out the promise of its motto: **"Helping Educators Do Their Work Better."**